Teaching
From the
Deep
End

Foreword by William Ayers

Teaching
From the
Deep
End

**Succeeding With
Today's Classroom
Challenges**

*This is going to be
a terrific year for you!
Good luck!*

Dominic Belmonte

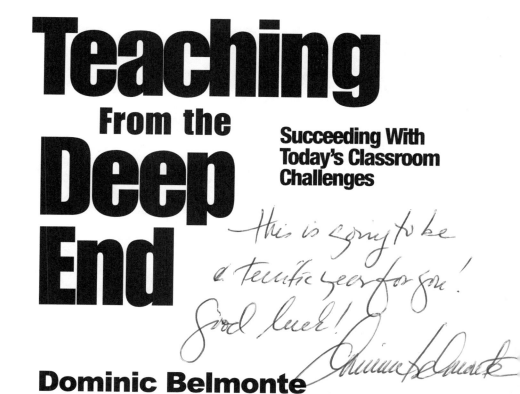

CORWIN PRESS, INC.
A Sage Publications Company
Thousand Oaks, California

Illustrations by Jim Pudlewski, Crete, Illinois

For information:

Corwin Press, Inc.
A Sage Publications Company
2455 Teller Road
Thousand Oaks, California 91320
www.corwinpress.com

Sage Publications Ltd.
6 Bonhill Street
London EC2A 4PU
United Kingdom

Sage Publications India Pvt. Ltd.
B-42 Panchsheel Enclave
Post Box 4109
New Delhi 110 017 India

Printed in the United States of America

Library of Congress Cataloging-in-Publication Data

Belmonte, Dominic.
Teaching from the deep end : succeeding with today's classroom challenges / Dominic Belmonte.
    p. cm.
Includes bibliographical references and index.
ISBN 0-7619-3848-6 (Cloth) — ISBN 0-7619-3849-4 (Paper)
    1. Teaching-United States. 2. Teachers-Training of-United States.
I. Title.
LB1025.3 .B455 2003
371.102—dc211
                        2002154677

03 04 05 06 10 9 8 7 6 5 4 3 2 1

Acquisitions Editor:	Faye Zucker
Editorial Assistants:	Julia Parnell and Stacy Wagner
Production Editor:	Melanie Birdsall
Copy Editor:	Robert Holm
Typesetter:	C&M Digitals (P) Ltd.
Proofreader:	Theresa Kay
Indexer:	Teri Greenberg
Cover Designer:	Tracy Miller
Production Artist:	Michelle Lee

Contents

Foreword

A teacher's life is tough. Don't kid yourself with dreams of sweetness and light, of admiring colleagues, compliant children, and grateful parents. Step into your classroom and you will be entering the abyss. Like diving into the deep end of a pool filled with icy water—the plunge will be heart-stopping.

Dominic Belmonte is the guardian angel whom the luckiest of us meet when we're ready to take that plunge. If the teacher's career is a journey, then Dom is the guide who interprets not only the breathtaking drops and the arduous uphill climbs, but also the countless sights of surprising beauty all along the way. Stay with it, Dom will urge, and then he will offer a thousand practical ideas for reaching the next plateau. He's been there, and it shows—every bit of advice is borne of the pain as well as the bliss of a life lived with passion and purpose, a life in teaching. Dom has built rich, exciting classrooms for kids year after year, and for over a decade he has led efforts to recruit talented young people into teaching and designed programs to ignite their hearts, fire their minds, and develop their capacity to be the best.

Stay with it, he will say again, through sulk and sob and crankiness; stay with it and you, too, can achieve a kind of nobility. There's heart here, a kind of benighted zealotry, exactly what's needed to rescue us from our discontents and to bring teaching into focus as the ethical enterprise it really is.

Good teaching finds its truest footing on the practice of profound respect—respect for children as three-dimensional and sacred beings, respect for their families, respect for one's calling and one's self, respect for all of life and for the wider world. Nourishing the capacity for the practice of respect is foundational in teaching. It involves learning to resist the toxic habit of labeling that pervades our schools, to see into the hearts and minds and souls of the dynamic, actual students who enter our classrooms, to identify them as three-dimensional, complex, in-motion, and each one special, even sacred. It means finding assets in families and communities where others see only deficits. And it means a bold engagement with the world, a world in desperate need of repair to be sure, but the only world we've got after all.

Students are not inert bits of matter awaiting our various ministrations but are rather unruly sparks of meaning-making energy, each on a quest for his or her own humanity. Those of us who teach cannot think of ourselves as clerks or bureaucrats but rather must ourselves be in-motion, on a quest for wholeness as well.

Nurturing the ability to see and to feel things from a range of other perspectives is vital in this journey—a bigot, after all, may be thought of as someone whose imagination has atrophied. Teachers cannot afford bigotry, and so they need to develop big imaginations. Learning to listen actively with the possibility of being changed is part of it; learning to speak forcefully but respectfully with the hope of being heard is another part. This means creating opportunities for lateral communication, the public space for dialogue in our classrooms.

Education is an arena of hope and struggle—hope for a better future, a more humanistic society, a peaceful and just world, and struggle over whom and what to include, and the meaning of the good life. School is where questions of identity—Who in the world am I?— and questions of justice—What in the world are my choices and my chances?—are enacted and worked out in their dailyness.

Teaching is the calling of callings, the calling that opens the doors to an infinite array of choices and possibilities for others. Dom Belmonte calls us to be at our best. In this, he is our engaging angel, our guide, our necessary teaching fellow.

—William Ayers
Distinguished Professor
University Scholar
College of Education
The University of Illinois at Chicago

Preface

So I wrote what follows for my daughter, Mary Beth, and my son, Nic, so they could see.

I wrote what follows for the three people most responsible for helping me acquire the teaching passion: Bill Gorgo in high school with his knobby sweaters and scraggly beard and his movement from painting to album to poem to novel to sculpture to opera always saying, "See? See?" To the late Paul Carroll, a poet who spoke in the rain to angels and could hit consecutive three point jumpers and pointed to the poem and said to me, "See? See?" And to the poet Mike Anania who encouraged and taught me how to question so my students could say "Aha" as I said "See?"

I wrote what follows for my late father and the words we said in time and for teaching me then and always now what to value, how to hold.

I wrote what follows for my mother and her endless love and devotion to the always simple and right thing.

I wrote what follows for the great teachers I have worked with throughout my career, especially all who have worked at York Community High School in Elmhurst, Illinois, where from 1976–1996 I was patiently mentored then helped to patiently mentor a new generation of teachers.

I especially dedicate what follows in memory of my dear friend, Jerry Lombardo, who inspired a generation of students with his passion for music and his steadfast belief in the goodness of all children. He passed much too soon without one written word about the nature of his talent. As William Blake wrote, "We are put on earth a little space/So that we may learn to bear the beams of love." Indeed.

I wrote what follows to all the students I've helped and who've helped me. Thank you for the love I hardly ever deserved and the laughter and the tears and the moments when we knew something special was unfolding and just went with it for all of our benefit.

I wrote what follows for all the students I've failed by my own word or deed. I remember each and every one of you and hope you're well and successful.

I wrote what follows for the Fellows of the Golden Apple Foundation and for Mike and Pat Koldyke. These two brave and generous people gave a teacher at the end of his career rope the belief that what he did had merit, and for those unique individuals they similarly touched, for the things we helped create because of that confidence.

And I wrote what follows for my wife Mary Lee, for the life and ineffable strength her love gives me.

ACKNOWLEDGMENTS

I am grateful to Bill Ayers for being the first to read this manuscript, see value in it, and help it to find its audience. Bill is a rare and generous soul who continues to help others find meaning in their lives through teaching and who displays uncommon courage and tenacity in his beliefs.

I thank my colleagues, Kathy Wandro and Penny Lundquist, who read the drafts and offered much appreciated encouragement early on in its development. For further suggestion and much needed validation I thank Drew Bendelow, Peg Cain, Greg Michie, Dr. Penelope Peterson, Jim Pudlewski, who graciously illustrated this text, and especially Cissy Sullivan, whose comments touched my heart.

Most of all, I am grateful to Faye Zucker of Corwin Press for her steadfast encouragement and gentle guidance of this manuscript past its original raucous stream of consciousness to something akin to rational thought. That this effort rests in your hands is due to Faye's deeply appreciated tenacity. I hope you find within it utility.

Corwin Press thanks the following reviewers for their contributions to this work:

Rob Bocchino, Heart of Change; Change of Heart, Associates; Baldwinsville, NY.

Sandra Hildreth, Adirondack Wilderness Landscapes, Norwood, NY.

Diane Holben, Saucon Valley High School, PA.

Fred MacDonald, Ontario College of Teachers, Ontario, Canada.

Susan Mintz, Curry School of Education, University of Virginia, Charlottesville, VA.

Jolinda Simes, Minneapolis Public Schools, Minneapolis, MN.

Penelope Swenson, California State University, Bakersfield, CA.

About the Author

 **Dominic Belmonte** taught at York Community High School in Elmhurst, Illinois, for 20 years as an English teacher and Chairman of the English Department. He now serves the Golden Apple Foundation for Excellence in Teaching as its Director of Teacher Preparation. A member and past chairman of the Golden Apple Academy of Educators, in 1989 he co-created the Golden Apple Scholars of Illinois program, a pre-induction teacher preparation experience which is now the Golden Apple Foundation's largest program. A 2001 study of the Scholars program conducted by the University of Illinois at Chicago proved participation in the Scholars program a significant factor in improving the preparedness of its participants. Harvard University named the Scholars program as one of 15 programs out of 1,200 nationwide as a finalist for its Innovations in American Government award. In 1996 Dom also co-created the GATE (Golden Apple Teacher Education) program, an alternative pathway to teacher certification for mid-career adults wishing a career in teaching secondary math or science or elementary school children. He may be reached via e-mail at dbelmonte@goldenapple.org

CHAPTER ONE

The Teaching Profession

*What Are You Doing
and Why Are You Doing It?*

Here are three truths about teaching:

1. There exists in this country a resilient core of spectacular teachers who deserve the title "teacher." Their very lives serve to instruct, energize, and inspire a generation of students.

2. There exists in this country another resilient core of teachers. This group does not inspire, does not teach well, and responds dismally to the challenge of educating children.

3. The educational community needs to find millions of new teachers who represent the first truth, and there is very little the educational community can do about those representing the second truth.

The United States faces a national teacher shortage and that provides an opportunity to improve our preparation of the next generation of teachers. We can hope to increase the likelihood that our children, especially children in urban, rural, and less advantaged school settings, can find themselves in the company of talented

1

teachers. We know that consecutive experiences with teachers of quality can help children overcome the disadvantages of poverty. We also know the damaging effect a string of less than excellent teachers can have on the development of children.

We must acquire a new generation of quality teachers. We must do this in the face of a national perception of our profession as less desirable than other professions. We must do so in a nation that pays lip service to the importance of teaching but provides little in the way of resources such as competitive salaries, professional working conditions, practitioner input on the development of curricula and school management, and professional advancement. Often treated as children—forbidden to use a phone, required to ask permission to duplicate copies—teachers of twenty years' experience sadly realize they hold the identical responsibility as first-year teachers, and their expertise and experience generally are not sought to better their schools.

Despite these challenges, we must acquire this new generation of quality teachers. While legislators and pundits endlessly debate the many problems that we as teachers are not empowered to solve, we can still address one essential question central to quality teaching: How does one acquire the authority to stand in front of children as a teacher of substance and dimension? This authority does not derive from the power of the grade book or the crossly phrased word, and certainly it is not authority by demand. So how does one acquire the ability to become a great teacher?

I submit what follows as one path to the goal of quality teaching. It derives from the stuff and substance of a career in education, of learning how to teach, of reflection on improving my teaching, of imparting what I learned to others. It is based on the experiences I had in the classroom, as an administrator, and as the co-creator of two programs in Illinois that recruit and prepare teachers, one by augmenting traditional preparation for undergraduates (the Golden Apple Scholars of Illinois) and the other by offering an alternative pathway to teaching for mid-career adults (GATE, Golden Apple Teacher Education). My quest individually and as part of the Golden Apple Foundation has been to advance the teaching profession by recognizing excellent teachers, leveraging their thinking and efforts to improve education, recruiting and preparing prospective teachers, and providing all teachers with innovative resources. My goal is to see teaching perceived as a profession of honor that brings resilient and inspiring people into the lives of children who need resilience and inspiration.

How do we acquire a generation of quality teachers? Some misstate the process and call it teacher *training*. Dogs are trained. Teachers are prepared. Teacher preparation implies a journey, for becoming a teacher is a journey of thought and of action. A teacher must think about many things long before beginning to teach. A teacher must reflect before doing and after doing. That sounds simplistic, yet there is preparatory work that allows a teacher to *do,* involving thought and structure.

I have always wanted to write about the ideas and themes of the courses I have presented to prospective teachers. It has been a singular honor to help create pathways to teaching for both undergraduates and mid-career adults. This desire became even more acute when my daughter Mary Beth decided she wanted to teach high school English. It is certainly a unique feeling to have trod a certain path in one's professional life, then to glance behind to see your own child following it. While I am thrilled with her path, of course I worry for her as I worry for all who embark on the teaching journey.

We must provide a pathway to success for this new generation of quality teachers. We must work to raise perceptions about the value of the teaching profession in America. What follows is just as much for Mary Beth as it is for all of you who will read this book.

Twenty-five years in education has shown me that the process of becoming a teacher is very much the process of becoming a person. One grows into a stronger knowledge of what it means to be a teacher. One never finishes learning about how best to instruct and how best to inspire students. For those of you who wish to teach, for those of you who wish to inspire others to teach, for those of you young in the profession or those wanting to learn more—our time, by golly, has come.

Please interpret what follows as steps along a path, one that must be approached with passion. You must enter the classroom with passion—not with some wild and unfocused enthusiasm, but with a passion formed by

- *Knowing* what you want to accomplish,
- *Seeing* those around you in order to begin properly,
- *Planning* to bring your students to knowledge and understanding,
- *Anticipating* challenges to that plan.

This passion cannot be manufactured. You know when someone is faking it up there by the big desk. The students can spot it even faster. No one wants to be that kind of teacher, not even those whose fatigue and cynicism have led them to fake it.

So you must have passion, but your passion must be connected to a plan. The teaching passion involves three necessary questions you must always ask:

1. *What* are you doing?

2. *Why* are you doing it?

3. *How* can you improve how you do it?

Becoming proficient at answering the first two questions allows you to entertain the third. Having a clear knowledge of all three enables you to enter a classroom purposefully. That purpose directs you to package your knowledge and your plan in a compelling manner. That compelling manner gives you the necessary insight to look at your students. You thereby become a student of those students. That study allows you to proceed.

REFLECTIVE EXERCISE

For whom are you grateful? List those people and the gifts they have brought to you. Now examine that list. Does what you list define who you are? Is what you list reflected in your teaching?

Keep this list of gifts. What you list will in part define who you are, which will reflect how you teach.

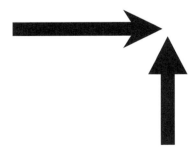

CHAPTER TWO

The Classroom

Where Teacher's Path
and Student's Path Converge

Turn back to the preceding page and look again at those arrows. Think of them as an approximation, like all images, of the reality you may have experienced on your pathway to becoming a teacher.

One line represents your life. Of course its path has not been arrow straight. The moments of your life that have defined you take years of reflection to unravel. Your learning, your reading and writing, the steps you took to acquire the intelligence you command, the person you are, none of these can be so easily represented. Yet pretend for a moment that one straight arrow can represent your path through life. You've come from a direction, traveled a path to where you are right now, holding this book and moving onward. Congratulations! You have made it this far on your journey, as wonder and hope drive you onward into the mystery of what's ahead.

The other arrow represents the pathways of the students you will meet, young people from different lives who have experienced different moments and have acquired different knowledge from those moments. All those youngsters, and all their moments, have gathered by fate and circumstance in the classroom you now or will soon sit in, waiting. Your separate lives have converged in this one place for an appointed time. When they enter the classroom and sit and look at you, then you will understand the image on the preceding page and its significance.

WILL YOU BE READY TO TEACH?

You have studied and you have learned. Your methodology class lurks somewhere nearby in your mind, but the theory you studied becomes the theory forgotten as the students now look at you with wondering, weighing eyes. Now you understand that you're in there for a reason. You wanted to do this, always wanted to be up front, in charge, and you believed being by the big desk put you up front and in charge. You know they are looking and you know they are weighing and so you must begin somewhere and somehow. Will you be ready?

There may come a time when one of them will die in circumstances tragic or senseless, and there will be one empty desk in a room full of eyes looking to you in fear for the answer and the reason. When that happens, will you be ready?

There may come a time when your words or deeds—the very thing you say or avoid saying, the very thing you do or decide not to do—will instruct or heal or ease or repair. You may be the one who gives a student a reason to go onward, a feeling that there is a reason for being—if you notice the moment and know how to respond to it. Those moments approach. Will you be ready?

There may come a time when a student sees in you something that can be trusted, something you may not even see in yourself. That student may ask, "Would you still like me if I were gay?" Or another student may tell you that she was pregnant but now she is bleeding or about the vile acts of family members or that Grandpa has to die and can you please help? You will remember that you were taught to teach verb tense and polynomials. But now can you help, should you help, how?

So many people are wary of being a teacher. They prefer pallid synonyms like "facilitator." This is not your fate. You want to teach because you know that more lives have been touched, and more lives have been saved, in the space between a teacher's desk and a student's desk than in any other: surgeon and patient, pastor and flock. This is no mere *sage on the stage* conceit. You want to be their teacher. You want to be ready.

HOW DOES ONE BECOME READY TO TEACH?

In the course of my time behind the big desk, I was engaged in the lives of some 3,500 young people. With some I failed miserably, with most it worked out. What I write about successful teaching may or may not be a template for you, but it will describe my passion, for I believe that only with passion can you succeed as a teacher. But passion alone is not the answer. If it were, then anyone could get up there. All the passion in the world for teaching children will not offer you success if you have little passion for or knowledge of subject content or teaching strategy. All the knowledge in the world about subject content will not help you if you have no passion for people.

The search for a balance between your passions will occupy you throughout your career. Few careers have as much at stake for so many as teaching. Air traffic controllers control hundreds of people by the very things they say and decide. But they do not see or smell them as they decide. The family physician heals by word and deed, and makes as many decisions of import. But few of them outside the operating room or the emergency room have to decide instantly about the right thing to do, in a crowd, the clock ticking. Police officers keep harmony and contend with a wide spectrum of life. But few of them have fifteen to thirty citizens together in one room demanding in their earnest way what you've been entrusted to provide.

My students from years ago occasionally return to say, "You remember when you said . . . ?" or "Remember when you wrote . . . ?" and "That really helped, thanks." In fact, I don't even remember what I had for breakfast that morning, but like Velcro the moments I had with them have been held, for good or naught. As teachers we have the power to create so much good or naught that if you think about it too long you freeze up, like trying to command your breathing. But you have to say something up there, don't you? Even when you hear the doubter in your head whisper "You're faking. They know." Soon, your paranoia reasons, the door will open and the principal or the truth police will pour in, and they will point you to the exit. Why didn't anybody in college tell you it was going to be this real, this raw, this critical?

Starting in 1976 I began to find purpose and meaning in my life by helping children find purpose and meaning in theirs. Through my errors, through my successes, and through the example of masterful teachers I was able to carve some beliefs about the craft and art of this noble but maligned profession. Teaching is noble for the thousands who have invested pure talent and honest reflection into creating classroom moments, inspiring children to believe that they can achieve and acquire knowledge and meaning on their own. Teaching is maligned because there are many who hold the rank of teacher but tarnish its integrity by callousness, cynicism, and incompetence. But you who read on, let us believe that bitterness will not ever be your fate. As you prepare or continue your craft, let me share with you some of my ways of holding this profession, offer you some teaching approaches to consider, show you some examples of my classroom successes and my classroom follies.

I have never laughed as hard as I have in a classroom, nor cried as bitterly, nor discovered so much I had yet to learn in the company of students.

Socrates is long dead, yet we still continue his method of imparting information and inspiring learning in a cloistered room with one person leading children in activities. This is called teaching.

Only those in the profession recognize its oddity. Do you remember your speech classes in high school? Standing in front of people, exposing all you are, what you look like, how you talk, how you think in front of a group of bored people not wanting to hear what you have to say? Within seconds after starting, that little voice in your head began to speak to you: *"They're looking at me. They know I have no idea what I'm talking about and they have no interest. I could spontaneously combust right here in front of them. Oh, why was I born?"*

Do thoughts like that seem too far-fetched? Wait until you stand in front of students, hundreds of them all day long. Five classes daily (if you're a high school teacher), 185 days or so per year, 50 minutes per class period: that's 45,000 minutes of class time. That's 15,000 three-minute speeches in one school year! Your students will sit because our culture prefers its students to sit while looking at you. You'll look at your students because our culture prefers its teachers to keep eyes opened when facing students. You'll open your mouth to speak because the primary communication medium our culture uses in the classroom is the spoken word. And within minutes you will have not only that voice inside your head judging you, but all your students as well.

The truth is that your students are always weighing and judging you, just like you did your own teachers. Remember when that poor teacher started class and you and your classmates knew within an instant whether you should start making that person miserable? Your students now will see within moments if you are a person of substance or a fraud. They will be able to distinguish genuine concern from fakery. Within a short while you will be sized up, rated, judged.

So why are you up there? *"You should have gone into real estate like your mother wanted,"* says that ever present voice at your ear. *"But no!"* There you are, up front, in charge. In a short time, your students will know whether you are someone they want to understand or withstand.

WHAT IS A TEACHER? A PARABLE

Envision an average city street, with curb and streetlight on the corner.

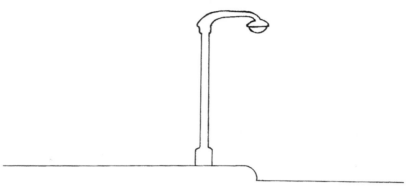

On that street corner, three persons converge. One person stands under the streetlight, merely waiting for something to happen.

Another person walks by, his head adorned with a hat. Not just any hat, but a *cool* hat, for this person is ultimate cool. People may be starving around him, but he is unconcerned. Hunger and despair abound, no problem. Cool Hat has no worries, need not see. All he does is walk down the street unconcerned, cool hat over his eyes.

The third person in our story now approaches behind the wheel of a car. Regardless of the circumstances, he approaches, fast.

Set the play in motion. Cool Hat walks down the street. Does he notice the person under the street lamp? Of course not. So cool and so unconcerned is he about all that is around him that he steps off the curb neither knowing nor seeing that Driver soon will turn him into a warm pool of protoplasm on the proverbial street.

But Person Under the Streetlamp sees the impending danger. And because Person sees, Person speaks. It need not be anything eloquent, not anything long, just a simple, "Heyyyyy! . . ."

. . . will do. And that's just enough for Cool Hat to stop, look up, note the car's approach, curse, and step out of the way. Away goes Driver, headed wherever. Cool Hat, his cool momentarily ruffled, readjusts his hat and, a bit more warily, continues his journey. And Person Under the Streetlamp remains.

This parable explains the reason for teaching. At various times we are all Cool Hat, blithely believing we can journey on without need of notice or care for anyone, comforted by the soft false assurance our cool hats provide. Lately I've been thinking it may be time to replace the cool hat symbol in this parable with an even more common symbol of modern isolation and unconcern, the portable CD player!

Nothing inside Cool Hat's head could have saved him from becoming that warm pool of protoplasm on the proverbial street. But it was what was inside the head of Person Under the Streetlamp that entered Cool Hat's head, and that activated Cool Hat, caused his reaction, saved him from harm. The ironic truth about Person Under the Streetlamp is that Person was under no obligation to say anything. But he did.

Person Under the Streetlamp is "teacher," the voices of all, living or dead, from whom we have learned, all the people in our lives who by the words they uttered brought us knowledge. Whether classroom teacher, parent, author, songwriter, poet, or playwright, the Person Under the Streetlamp is anyone whose words enter our minds in time to allow us to react, sometimes in time to avoid the full effect of injury from the Driver sitting behind the wheel of the Car of Life.

Our life journeys provide us with many cars hurtling toward us. For high school seniors, the most easily seen is the car called College. Many whom I've taught when they were big fish in the small pond of high school left for the University of Somewhere and the possibility of being flattened by the strength of the challenge that awaited them. For all of us, there will be an unavoidable car called Loss. How we recover and continue after that collision depends upon the quality of the words in our heads under our cool hats. Our teachers' words are the ones that allow us to move onward through our grief.

Teachers are the key to surviving. That's where you come in. You are Person Under the Streetlamp, waiting. You are under no obligation to provide anything for the Cool Hats who saunter past you for a time. But you know the Street and what it contains. And something within you compels you to utter words to the Cool Hats as they pass, and what you say and do may be what remains under their cool hats, allowing them to move forward further down the street, safely.

In *Catcher in the Rye,* Holden Caulfield hopes to protect his sister from falling off the cliff hidden in the rye field. Many of us in the profession see students sauntering innocently toward the cliff. Some need only a gentle whisper to draw them away from danger. Others seem to hurtle with full knowledge toward the cliff, shouting their desire to die. And we run after them, even though we have no obligation to do so, positioning ourselves before the cliff, helping them through their unhappy today to the brighter tomorrow their sadness and limited vision prevent them from seeing. Some students will fall no matter what you do, and the ones who fall will be the ones whose images stare back at you from the ceiling as you try to sleep.

Remember that responsibility the next time someone outside the profession lambastes you for taking off June, July, and August. Think about your critic standing in your shoes for a week, withering under your responsibility and challenge. You could certainly fare well in their jobs, staring at a computer screen or screaming numbers in a trade room. But after that your heart would ache for those moments in the company of children, where what you do and what you say mean so much.

REFLECTIVE EXERCISE

Complete one statement about what will always be true in your classroom. Try this:

    Regardless of what occurs in my life or in my school, in my classroom there will be always

_____

_____

_____.

Save this statement.

CHAPTER THREE

The Teacher's Words

You Can Heal and You Can Harm

Words are the inescapable vehicle by which the teacher imparts, inspires, questions, appraises, and reflects to students. All teachers would be wise to acquire a healthy command of and respect for words.

I heard about research done in the 1960s that determined that the average seventeen-year-old has a working command of 15,000–20,000 words. Now how they performed this study has always mystified me. Did they take an average seventeen-year-old, sit him or her in a room with paper and pen, and command, "Write every word you know!" How would such a teen respond? The cynic in me envisions the list: *"a, and, the, dude, party . . . "* and so on.

Over 1 million words in the English language, and regardless of our years of experience or education, each of us commands just a fraction of those words. But the things done with them!

WORD ALCHEMY

Example: Ordinarily, masses of students pass each other in school hallways each day. Some mutter "Hi" or "Hello" or "Yo" causing nary a pause save a smile or a nod. But if *that* person, you know, the answer to one's prayers, the person who could make life complete, walks past with an "I like your hair today," well, observe the reaction. The heart races, the sweat glands open, the tongue thickens, and

13

the student garumphs a response, all which is code for *I am noticed! That person is here! Let us rejoice!* The words echo throughout the school day and then sing out through the evening through telephone cables and across cyberspace. *I am noticed! That person is here! Let us rejoice!* All for words.

Every word has its history—fascinating in its development and use. Consider the anarchists who needed to ingest hashish before carrying out murderous attacks against political leaders. They became known as the "hashish eaters," in Arabic *hashshashin,* creating our present-day word "assassin." Of somewhat lesser import, consider the Middle Dutch phrase *wijssegger,* or wise speaker, origin of the American *wiseacre.* The history of words can fascinate.

Our minds contain the histories of the words we know and use. Experiment—watch how easy this is to enact. Ready? *Bear.* Ping! Into your mind comes the image. I'll refine and specify: *white bear.* Ping! There it is. Now stop thinking about white bear—no more white bear. Yet for awhile you'll wander to other paragraphs thinking and seeing "*white bear . . . white bear . . . .* "

Now think *yellow.* Your mind dutifully provides history: a color, a pejorative term implying cowardice. Perhaps some symbols appear, for example, the sun, or a songbird. Now take another word, one with its own separate history and place it alongside: *yellow . . . snow.* Ping Ping! You now see a third image appear, an image that wasn't in *yellow* or in *snow,* but in their juxtaposition. Yellow snow—that which you should not . . . Yes!

Word juxtaposition creates images that were not there in the words by themselves. Not only can these positions create images, they can evoke physical reaction as well. Consider: *bloody pus*—your mind images and makes you think "Yuck!" Or *uneven teeth*—your mind images and tempts you to judge a person so described. So powerful are words that their placement can create image and convey mood.

Now think about the images created and the moods conveyed in class by the words, "Darlene, that was a stupid thing to say." Or the words "Shut up!" which certainly convey to the student listening more than the order to become quiet.

Think of the unkind things teachers have said to you over the course of your schooling. You may not remember much about the subjects they taught, but if a teacher said something hurtful to you 15 years ago, you remember it chapter and verse. Sadly, the unkind things said to students often return as self-fulfilled prophecy. Told you're dumb, you'll think so. Told women can't achieve in math, it'll happen. But consider this: Tell students that they have a purpose in life, and they'll acquire one. Tell them that they can, and they will. Show them that they can, and they will surpass. The very words you use as a teacher can heal and cause success to happen. The very words you use as a teacher can cause harm and limit potential. The very words you use.

During my early teaching years, I taught summer school classes for juniors who had failed English 11. Given the freedom to do what I wanted, I presented the curriculum I had used for the Honors English 11 class. The summer school students read the poems, wrote the papers, succeeded. At the end of the summer term, I told them they had achieved with honors material. "But we're dumb," one confessed, almost as a shield as well as a wound. "Someone told you that," I replied, "and lied."

The power of words is in your hands as a teacher. With words, you can heal and you can harm. The children in your classrooms are well versed in the use of words as missiles, fully aware of the harm they cause in shouting *"fag, bimbo, dumb blonde, geek, drama queen."* You should strive to make your classroom a zone free from harmful words.

Words. Respect them and use them with knowledge of what they can do.

WORDS AS CONTRACT IN SOCIETY AND IN THE CLASSROOM

Words also denote a contractual arrangement. As a student, you most likely spent many cold mornings or afternoons waiting for a school bus to pick you up. The bus driver did indeed pick you up, even though no power forced him or her to do so. The bus driver could have entered the vehicle thinking, "Today, I will go to the dunes!" and could have driven past the cold and shivering students shouting "Today, the dunes!" But the driver stopped, greeted, transported. Why? Words.

You say to a student, "See me after your last class." That student's future is now altered. No longer can she travel with friends over to the mall after school, because you altered her future. If the student arrives and you aren't there, she will look at you funny the next day as you apologize and say, "Really, come by afterwards today." Be not there again, and you are deemed untrustworthy. Your contract is not good. Why? Words.

You walk among your students. They sit in rows perfectly confident that you are not going to take a swing at any of them, even though you have the power to do so, even though you may harbor the desire to do so. But they sit perfectly comfortable in the unspoken agreement. You will not harm them, even though you could. Why? Words.

The bus driver signed a contract with implied words that on specific days at specific locations, all those who look like they're heading for school will be picked up and transported. You signed a contract with society, whether actual or implied, that allows you access to children in the promise that you will not harm them. So you do not. Your word is your contract.

We exist as a society by means of an amazing irony. We live in freedom by voluntarily giving up our freedom. We have the freedom to hit, but we do not. We have the freedom to drive to the dunes on a workday, but we do not. We have the freedom to drive through red lights, but we do not.

The very notion of civil disobedience is predicated on people activating the freedoms they have but normally suppress. Your students do not move en masse out the door of your classroom before the bell rings, even though they have the freedom to do so, and probably at times harbor the desire. What prevents them all from leaving? Nothing.

If they were particularly incensed at some injustice that occurred at school, they could walk out in protest, march to the nearest intersection, and sit down in the street, arms locked. If they were to act on their freedom to do just that, the cars approaching them would have the freedom to run them over, but would not act on that freedom even if gridlock ensued. If gridlock were to ensue, police would be called in to clear the intersection, arresting those who refuse to move while news helicopters hover overhead. Then the arrested would have to be processed, overburdening the local police station or courthouse. The entire free flow of society might grind to a halt to accommodate those who act on the freedom they ordinarily relinquish in order to be a part of society.

Similarly, the society of your classroom depends upon a voluntary relinquishing of freedom. It is up to you to help foster meaning and peace and safety and dimension within your classroom. That is your contract. We have the freedom to choose chaos, but we crave order. We have the freedom to lie, but we strive for truth.

WORDS AS MAPS TO THE
TERRITORY OF YOUR CLASSROOM

Our words create maps of the territory others experience. In *Language in Thought and Action* ([1949] 1991), a semantics text seminal in the development of my teaching, S. I. Hayakawa discussed the map-territory distinction. It is a strong basis upon which to understand the power of words as they relate to your position as a teacher.

To simplify Hayakawa's semantic perception: *maps* are words that attempt to define the *territory* of reality. Maps are not the territory itself; rather they are approximations of the territory, since our perceptions of reality differ and our words do not exactly reflect the reality of life.

We grow up and learn life by means of a series of "maps" presented to us of how the world works. The maps come from those closest to us, those we encounter, what we read, what we experience. Trouble is, many of our maps are false representations of reality, and we go through life trying to rework the false maps we are given. This is the key reason prejudice exists, a matter I'll reserve for closer discussion in Chapter 9.

Like many of you, I have participated in the deliberate creation of false maps, sometimes knowingly and lovingly. When my wife and I gave our daughter the false map known as "Santa Claus," it was with a desire to extend to her a belief in the love and generosity of the world. Then came that damn day when she brought home the word from her fellow third graders. "Mom, Dad," she sniffed at the dinner table, "the kids at school told me there's no Santa Claus. Isn't there?"

My wife and I looked at each other with the "here we go" knowing look that our false map made inevitable. I tried to use my wordsmith powers to extend her childhood a little more: "Well, Mary Beth, if you took all the love in the world and gave it a human face, Santa's would be that face." Not bad, right? Of course, she saw through it instantly.

"But Dad, is there?" Another look from my wife indicated that now I was on my own, so there I went, into that dark place where map and territory collide. "No dear, there really isn't."

"Boo-hoo!" wailed my daughter, bolting from the table and running upstairs to bed. "Boo-hoo!" sobbed my wife, running after her to spend the night with her daughter's tears. And Dad remained alone with the unfinished meal pondering the sad world of map-territory displacement.

The next morning, my swollen-eyed daughter and I hid from each other behind cereal boxes. Her attack was simple, yet relentless. "Dad, the Easter Bunny?" I wished for a larger box of cereal. "Uh, no, honey." "The tooth fairy?" Sigh and double sigh: "No, baby, no tooth fairy either." Then she became indignant: "God?" "Well yes, baby, in our house, there is God."

In measures small and large, what you do in the classroom creates maps for your students representing your perception of the territory you are teaching. Hayakawa believed that words impart two things: a body of knowledge and a way of holding that body of knowledge.

The words that you use create not just maps for your students. They also represent a contractual arrangement. Even though no power compels them, your students for the most part will remain in your classroom and will pay attention to you unless and until you give them a reason to abandon caring about you. And you will remain with them, voluntarily giving up your freedom to be elsewhere, presenting to them through words both a body of knowledge and a way of holding the body of knowledge you wish them to discover.

Your every word and action, as well as your every silence and inaction, will communicate meaning to your students. I hope your words match reality as accurately as a map describes a territory. When given the choice, I hope you choose words that heal, clarify, support, and inspire. I hope your words are contractually sound. But before they can be, you must know your reasons for standing by the big desk at the front of the classroom.

REFLECTIVE EXERCISE

List the words you know never to use in front of students. I know you won't curse in front of them, so think deeper, to the words you know could hurt or limit them. Make a small sign with those words in a crossed circle. Paste them in your grade book. Give $100 to your favorite charity every time you falter.

CHAPTER FOUR

The Teaching Persona

Who You Are When You're
Standing Up There by the Big Desk

In Robert Penn Warren's novel *All the King's Men,* the main character Jack Burden muses as he drives in the rain about all the "you's" he has portrayed in his life. The person he was in school was not the person he was in the story's present, running political cover for his Louisiana governor. The person he was with his former wife was not the person he was with his childhood sweetheart and forever lover. The person he was in the car at that time driving alone in the rain resembled none of the other manifestations of himself. Who was the real one?

This sort of musing is Basic Irony 101. In *Language in Thought and Action* ([1949] 1991), S. I. Hayakawa recognizes the differences in what we project to others as our understanding of different semantic environments. We present ourselves to different people differently. We do not speak to our pastor as we do to our spouse. We do not use street slang in the work place. We do not speak to our parents as we do our friends. We know how to adjust our language to fit the environments in which we find ourselves. And we know how to adjust our *selves* to fit our environments. We change ourselves as easily as we change our shirts.

Are these other selves false images? Or are they rather facets of the person we are, revealed by specific circumstances? When we adjust and when we alter, we are not donning false maps any more than we are different when we change clothes. We respond to circumstances and show a facet of ourselves appropriate to a specific environment.

How You Present Yourself in Your Classroom

This discussion leads us to consider how you will present yourself in your classroom. Many novice teachers believe they must ruthlessly omit all aspects of their personality to present Teacher Animatron who does not smile until some holiday passes. Others believe only an absolutely faithful presentation of one's true self is honest enough. Both impressions have their faults.

To show little of yourself to your students clouds your effectiveness. But if you present yourself "warts and all" to your students, you will also, ironically, lose effectiveness. Your personal life will sometimes weigh heavily upon your ability to work. As department chair, I once walked past a colleague's classroom and observed her weeping in front of her ninth grade students. Under certain circumstances, showing emotion is appropriate, but my instincts led me to enter the room that day and ask if she wished me to sit with her students while she left the room to compose herself. Later, she divulged that she had been detailing part of her marital discord and impending divorce to her students when her emotions got the better of her. My response was part sharp, part compassionate: What did she hope to gain by presenting her emotional pain to 14- and 15-year-olds, some of whom were doubtless dealing with their own emotional pain? What did she hope to receive from them? Advice? Sympathy? Were they equipped to offer either? Should they be expected to provide either?

What students look for in their teacher is a combination of sensitivity and strength. We adults all deal with the challenges of life: our aging, the aging of those we love, love's inconstancy, disappointment, betrayal, isolation, separation, and death. Should we project our struggle with all these challenges to the children we teach? Will that prepare them for the disappointments they will face as adults?

The persona we project to our students as teachers is an amalgam of who we are. The classroom is a semantic environment where we mix hope and struggle. Your students need to see you as someone who has reached a point of triumph over travail, both academic and personal, while continuing to cope with the pressures of life. Your presence in front of them serves as a role model of potential they can look to for hope for their own struggles. This does not mean that you do not show concern or doubt. But neither should you reflect hopelessness or futility, even if you are besieged by such demons. If you let them, your students will feed off your negativity as surely as they will acquire nurture from your energy and your strength.

How many times can you recall a teacher you admired having a "dark day" and the deleterious effect that mood had on the entire class? The unease that teacher brought into the classroom contributed little to education for that day. So your persona as teacher animates the atmosphere of your classroom. Learning how to compartmentalize your life so that its challenges are set aside while you are with your students is neither lie nor hypocrisy, but realistic and professional. You can choose to hold the welfare of your students over your own welfare each day. Some may call that fakery or acting, but in fact it is merely an amalgam of your true self, a facet directed toward the lights of your students' minds to help them with their own life path.

There is a further, practical advantage to your developing a teaching persona. It can provide an appropriate boundary for those times when students clamor for more information about you, perhaps to extend sympathy or to delay an assignment. "Tell us about the sixties," was, for teachers of my generation, an invitation to slip into the nostalgic haze of youth. But are there not some questions that you might not want to answer: "Did you take drugs then?" "Do you now?" "Did you live with a lover?" "Do you now?" "Did the FBI collect information about you?" "Were you ever arrested?" Such questions, even if innocently asked, can paint the teacher into a corner if the teacher is overly concerned about detailing a "true" self.

Familiarity with students has its limits, and it is unnecessary and inappropriate in the name of honesty to reveal a great amount of detail about your past or your present. The teacher who goes overboard in disclosing personal detail, to the point that it may seem to students that the teacher's life is part of the curriculum, is demonstrating a narcissism that does not equate with effective teaching. The "sage on the stage" teaching persona must be moderated to allow the students in the classroom to have their own actions and their struggles championed.

So how do you go about constructing your teaching persona? Is it like studying acting or speech?

HOW YOU ASK QUESTIONS

Key elements in the development of your teaching persona are

- The way you ask questions,
- The kinds of questions you ask,
- The philosophic stance you evince to your students as you ask questions.

I believe asking questions is an art form, one that requires diligent practice and skill.

As a novice teacher, you may start out much the way I did, with a prepared list of questions. I recall with sad nostalgia my first year as a teacher, when I asked my prepared questions and received answers, or silence, or what I thought were erroneous answers. I read through my list of questions, looked up at their end, and noted with nervousness that much time remained and I had no idea where to go. Perhaps the following suggestions will save you some of those awkward moments.

Don't advertise that you know the answer to every question you ask. Even if you have studied the topic of the day until you feel as if you coined the idea yourself, try not to show an "I know it, you don't, and I will ask questions until your thoughts match mine" mode. That stance reduces question-asking to a tiresome game that does not promote thought. I aimed to approach a subject with an earnest befuddlement—not so extreme as to suggest I was a dolt on the subject, but abundantly clear that in the investigation of a topic, we were discovering answers together. This tack will be difficult if you have the kind of personality that must always know and project that superiority. If that is your personality, then you have already projected it in your classroom, and your students will be loathe to consider questions if you already know the answer.

Use the answer of one student to prompt the next question. "Tom, what Janet says about this topic has some merit. Does it match what you felt about this subject?" Rather than lean on a prepared list of questions, weave new questions out of the fabric of your students' answers.

Don't be afraid of silence. Novice teachers often get skittish about silence and proceed to answer all their own questions, thereby cueing students on how the class will work—just allow the teacher to ask and answer without interference or participation. If you find yourself confronting silence, I would recommend looking at the kind of questions you are asking. Do they require mere repetition of material, or do they ask the students to move to deeper levels? Do you see the difference between the question, "Where are the letters to Celie hidden in *The Color Purple?*" and the question, "Is it wrong under every circumstance to keep letters from someone? What if your parent wanted to hide something from you? Is that always wrong?"

Do not ask questions that make students defensive. "What did you think of the book?" you ask. "I hated it," someone responds. "Why did you hate it?" "Because I did, that's why" is the likely and appropriate response. Such questions make students defend themselves for fear of being made to look a fool. Avoid such questions. Liking or not liking something is not the highest level of discussion to consider. Finding the relevant connection to the student's life is the more appropriate goal.

Avoid questions that begin with "What about . . . ?" These are questions with circular answers. The appropriate retort will be "Well, what about it?"

Avoid false praise. Praise responses that strike you as sound, but do not praise every sentence your students utter. Students are remarkably adept at detecting false praise. They will pick up on insincere and indiscriminate praise as readily as they will someone who absolutely cannot offer positive comment to anyone. In either extreme lies disregard and disrespect for students.

Be aware of how you choose respondents. My colleagues were always amazed when I noted that they asked more questions of males than of females, or that they called on students predominantly on one side of the room over the other. Become aware of your patterns.

Always let them talk! Do not be a slave to the tyranny of coverage, of time constraints, of what's next on your lesson plan. When the hands go up, let them answer. Weave their answers to the next point, praise, and avoid the pontification gene in you that wishes to get them to where you want them to be by telling them what you think. The point is to let them get there, not by your force, but by their discussion. So get out of their way. The absolute best part of classroom discussion is when they take it over, leaving you to be the adroit and focused air traffic controller who directs speaking order. Don't say, "Okay, this is the last comment we'll take on this subject—we have to keep moving." Stay on their schedule, not yours.

Become a student of the art of asking questions as a way of opening your students to discussion and to critical thinking.

How You Decorate Your Classroom

Your teaching persona is also revealed in the educational atmosphere you foster. The way in which you organize and adorn your room, if you are fortunate to have your own classroom, offers many messages to children.

Many new teachers are itinerant travelers, bravely chugging along the halls with their stuff in tow on a cart of some kind. It's an awful way to treat professionals and if it happens to you, I hope you get a room of your own next year, even if you have to share with another teacher. When you have actual wall space, then you have the opportunity to make your room reflect your teaching tenets (more about tenets in Chapter 6). In this manner, elementary teachers have an understanding stronger than their secondary colleagues, many of whom never bother with anything but the simplest of wall decor, like fire drill instructions or a sports team poster.

Your classrooms should be as well thought out as your lesson plans. Classroom decor will give your students something to stare at while feigning interest in what you're doing and still allow them to be engaged in something associated with the philosophy you have devised. The best teachers work in the most fascinating environments, rich in stimuli and complicated in design, some with and some without riches in technology or resources. The classrooms that demonstrate care and creativity have a design and a purpose. Such teachers know how children perceive and engage.

You can look around your own school for the creative and intriguing teachers. Ask the children—they'll tell you instantly who has captivated them. Then look at the surroundings of that teacher's room and watch her work. Note the persona she projects and ask her later what animates and inspires her teaching. You will always receive a well-articulated sense of mission animating a clearly reflected persona. The excellent teacher does not free-form a lesson like an improvised jazz riff. The great teacher does not work off the cuff. He or she proceeds as a result of inspired reflection and dogged practice.

"TELL ME WHAT YOU THINK OF ME": RECOGNIZING AND UNDERSTANDING YOUR TEACHING PERSONA

In a darkened room, 30 prospective teachers sit in a half circle. In the center of the room, lit by a lone light, a single chair is placed. A volunteer stands, walks to the chair, and faces the room. After stating his or her name, the volunteer asks, "Tell me what you think of me," and sits in the chair.

Once seated, the volunteer cannot speak. Those who are gathered around are instructed that they are free to respond or not to respond to the question. If responding, they must do so in complete sentences. After a prescribed interval, a moderator calls "time." The seated one then rises, saying only "thank you." The next one volunteers and the process is repeated.

This activity has been the culminating exercise in my work with prospective teachers for over two decades. I refer to it as the LaSalle exercise because I first experienced it at a religious retreat at LaSalle Manor in Plano, Illinois. I use it now not for religious revelation but to guide prospective teachers. They have studied the teaching profession as an art form. They have witnessed teaching styles that range from awesome to awful through their school site observations. They have brought their preconceived notions about what it means to teach and their preconceived notions about race and gender and children. Through the conversations and arguments and reflection, they are brought to a chair, to ask others what they think of them.

This exercise reverses the presumed power polarity in a class-room. The person up front, supposedly singular and powerful, wields no power and cannot speak once seated in the chair. The gathered, usually perceived as submissive to the will of the teacher, hold in their hands the self-esteem of the one seated.

Can you imagine any of your teachers in such a chair, in such a position? The tension is palpable, yet those in the room are drawn to volunteer. These prospective teachers want so much to be up there, by the big desk, in charge. This moment challenges that desire.

What occurs around that chair can be breathtaking, life chang-ing, and hard to describe unless witnessed. The gathered tell the one seated, in honest and humble tones, what they have seen. The gath-ered hold their power as it should always be held, gingerly and respectfully. Hope abounds. Honest advice is given. Colleagues form bonds that continue throughout their teaching careers. Copious tears are shed, as is appropriate whenever professionals engage in a risky activity and are rewarded with useful information for the next stage of their development as teachers.

TEACHER AS "TRAVELER"

Novice teachers and prospective teachers need to see the time they spend preparing to enter their profession as preparation for a jour-ney. Like all journeys, it involves arduous circumstances and unex-pected obstacles. The journey uncovers truths about the traveler, some unpleasant and in need of attention. The journey is a discovery of self in the company of others who cannot abide narcissism and cannot dwell in the company of self-conscious inaction. The traveler must learn all he or she can, including the wisdom that learning about the journey never ceases.

The traveler also must see the signs in the faces of the children entrusted to her. She must interpret the teachable moments, respect the important silences, and know how to respond to both. The trav-eler learns how to enter the moment, affect those within the moment, and leave the moment when appropriate. The traveler plans a lesson but is not slavishly devoted to the lesson to the exclusion of what is newly discovered along the way. The traveler sees, remembers what he saw, and cherishes all opportunities to have seen. As in all good journeys, a part of what was seen improves the traveler.

If the teacher traveler has done well, the students met and encountered along the way have fared even better. They discover they can learn. They discover they too must journey toward purpose and meaning. When warmer weather arrives and the best of that part of the journey is complete, the children continue elsewhere, and the traveler looks elsewhere for other children.

REFLECTIVE EXERCISES

1. Look back on the journey of your life. Can you hear the voices of your past? Can you hear the voices that shaped you, taught you, that gave you the tools to pursue the purpose and meaning for which you now search?

2. Now stretch your mind forward. Can you hear the voices of your future students? Can you hear their laughter, their questions, their anger, their joy, their thanks?

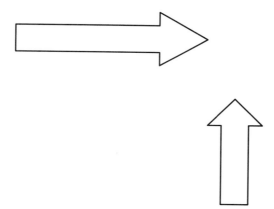

3. Next time you find yourself in conversation, try to step back and observe yourself. Do you appear natural and animated or stiff and formal? Do you dominate conversation or add to it?

4. Ask your friends about the way you project yourself in conversation. That is your first step to developing your own teacher persona.

CHAPTER FIVE

The Paperwork Can Kill You

In my vision of the almost perfect school, the key to teacher effectiveness would be every four teachers sharing an administrative assistant. In the business world, success is achieved through delegation. Not only is delegation good for business organization, it also ensures mental stability!

Only in the teaching world does one find a profession so insistent that everyone manage his or her own paperwork and handle every detail personally. Until you have entered this profession, you will not truly realize the immensity of the paperwork demands upon you, or how command of that paperwork will define your effectiveness to your administrators.

Here is a cruel truism: You can work with intensive concentration on improving your lesson plans, but if you keep sloppy grade books and attendance records you will seal your doom. You may have all your students excited about learning, but if you forget to send home notes to parents about immunization, then you will have a cross principal appearing at your classroom door.

You must devise a method of handling paperwork that will allow you to work on the most essential part of your job. I recommend triage, a term from medical practice, in which you sort by priority the paperwork that appears in your mailbox and deal with it in order of its importance.

GRADE BOOKS AND ATTENDANCE RECORDS

There are really only two parts of school paperwork you must place at absolute top priority: assigning grades in your grade book and keeping up-to-date attendance records. Both grade books and attendance records are legal documents that testify to the work you have done with your students, signified by a record of their academic progress, and a record of their daily presence or absence.

In my work with prospective teachers, I have found that inadequate work with the grade book and attendance keeping are the most serious threats to their continuing in the profession. You must assign work and that work must be adjudged and returned and recorded. You must show you know who is in front of you each day, and some schools may insist that you use arcane symbols to signify variations in a student's presence or absence: excused or unexcused, field trip absence, suspension, ill during class, parent picking up. In these matters, modeling can be a life-saver. Copy your mentor's approach if you have been assigned a mentor. If not, then ask the students who is the best in the building and befriend that teacher as a mentor.

STUDENT INFORMATION AND PARENT MESSAGES

After you have acquired a system you are comfortable with for grade books and attendance records, then move on to material about specific students (medical information, field trip forms, and so forth), followed by phone messages from parents.

These are the top four holy grails of teacher paperwork. No administrator will stand for sloppiness in grade books or attendance records. Colleagues who request information from you about your students will be miffed and spread that disdain to others if you do not reply to a counselor's request for information or homework assignments for absent students. No parent will stand for your not returning a phone message.

Almost everything else not directly relating to your students can be triaged until later. I used to gather all the "later" mail into a box to look at once a week. Of course, everyone who sends you paper believes it essential. But you have only four essentials:

1. grade books

2. attendance records

3. information about specific students

4. phone messages from parents

Everything else can wait.

The Paper Hill

Keeping your head above water when you feel like you're drowning in paper becomes yet another facet of teaching from the deep end. Since you cannot acquire administrative assistance, and you cannot stockpile the paperwork in your closet without attracting notice, you must devise systems that will recognize and prioritize. No teacher is ever recognized for outstanding handling of the candy forms or the overdue book announcements. But few teachers are recognized as stellar if they keep slovenly grade books or shoddy attendance records.

Good teachers are great at compartmentalizing their paperwork so it does not swallow them. Good texts exist on organizing the first weeks of school, on keeping records, on taking care of this part of the job so that you can focus your energy on the essentials.

Management of minutiae is itself an art form. Learn to copy the techniques of those whose work you admire. Learning from others is a vital task of the new teacher, and you won't succeed at this creative stealing and amalgamating if you stay in your room with the door closed. It may happen in your school building that you copy the questioning technique of one colleague, the assignments of another, the bulletin board ideas of a third, and the paperwork management of a fourth. Just beware that you may pick up a few bad habits while you're picking up the good ones. Stay alert.

Reflective Exercise

Triage your mail. Spend a few weeks separating the essential from the superfluous in your home mailbox. Pay a few bills on time and answer a few letters from friends. Then review your home-mail method template to duplicate or improve for your professional mail.

CHAPTER SIX

Your Educational Philosophy

Creating Your Teaching Tenets

Your longest pause as a teacher will follow reading the phrase found on employment applications new teachers fill out: *Describe your educational philosophy.* Quick: recite yours. Do you have one? You spent all that time in college reflecting about John Dewey. Meanwhile Johnny Dewey waits in your classroom and he cannot read and may have dyslexia besides a dysfunctional home life so how are you going to inspire Johnny—quick: recite.

This truly is the key to everything—why are you up there? What is your reason for teaching? This is the challenge new teachers find for themselves soon after September hellos fade to the workaday world. Your reliance on work sheets and your struggles with uncomfortable silences and hesitations and ebbing confidence are all the result of too little reflection on the essential question: *Why are you up there?*

You must have a reason. Your reason must connect to a belief system. You may be following a prescribed curriculum and that's fine. You may be forced to follow the pace of other teachers teaching the same subject or grade level and that's no sin. But why are *you* up there?

This you have to figure out before you start working. Your belief system will drive why you teach what you teach. That belief system can segment the curriculum you plan to teach into units that are subsets of the tenets you hold dear. Every lesson and/or experience you offer your class that refers back to the unit theme should also cohere to the tenets you hold.

Your tenets create the *frame* of your teaching. They give your teaching purpose and meaning. Without purpose and meaning, you are marking time and time will become your enemy. Without purpose and meaning, classroom silences and the inevitable mischief that follows will be your students' recognition that you don't know why you're up there. With a frame, your teaching will be clear and focused. If you hold the frame dear, your students will recognize the substance you project, and they will follow along. You may struggle mightily with classroom management and mark rules on the blackboard and study systems of classroom management, for which quite a cottage industry has arisen. But consider this: *no classroom management technique can be more effective than a teacher who knows why he or she is standing up there.*

Your teaching tenets should fit on a single page. Two decades of reflection on the teaching profession brought me 15 tenets. Everything I taught emanated from those phrases. I began all of my first classes, after the hearty hellos and the ever-traditional "Reading of the Names," with this one-sheet explanation of "This is what you will learn in here." Each of these principles was created over years of errors and perceptions, reflection, and experience. And they all point to one principle from which these tenets stemmed:

Barring pathology, any student, properly taught, can learn any subject.

The power of influence teachers wield is beyond perception. If you believe your students will achieve, they will, beyond their and your expectations. Limit their potential by what you hold in your mind about them, and you (not them, **you**) are responsible for that limitation.

I understand the arguments about students who come from disadvantaged homes, or are the victims of poverty and impoverished parenting. *But the potential each child holds can blossom or wither depending on a teacher's decision.* Remember this well: any time you say, or hear another teacher say, "These kids can't . . ." or "These kids won't . . . " what is really being said is "*I* can't," or more pathetically, "*I* won't."

Some of these tenets have already surfaced in earlier pages. Allow me to discuss some others and suggest how they can

FIFTEEN TEACHING TENETS

1. We are responsible for our actions. The consequences of our actions extend far beyond our ability to comprehend.

2. We are part of a legacy, and we can continue and improve that legacy.

3. If love is not the motivating factor in what you do, then why are you teaching?

4. Delay judgment. What seems often is not what is.

5. Never make any decision while exhausted or distracted.

6. We will never fully master this art of learning and living. In struggling to approach mastery, however, we achieve dignity and honor.

7. We must hold command of our learning as strongly as our regard for children. One without the other damages.

8. By understanding and accepting ourselves, we come to know.

9. Any teacher provides a body of knowledge. A good teacher provides a way to hold that body of knowledge.

10. We teach what we are far more than we teach what we teach.

11. More lives have been touched and more lives have been saved in the space between a teacher's desk and a student's desk than have ever been touched or saved in any other space.

12. The path to students' minds often passes directly across their hearts.

13. In responsible and creative risk-taking lies the beauty of accomplishment.

14. In what seems the most insignificant is often the most important.

15. In studying and trying to understand, we learn how to proceed.

influence your teaching. I suggest you must also craft your tenets and use them as the frame by which you present your lessons.

TENET: WE ARE RESPONSIBLE FOR OUR ACTIONS

This is the seat of my teaching passion, one which hard lessons and witnessing the lives of adolescents over two decades has presented to me. In his novel *All the King's Men,* Robert Penn Warren wrote of "the web of things" that interconnects us and from which we are all affected by the decisions we make. That lesson was reflected in many of the literary works I presented to my classes.

In Ray Bradbury's short story "The Sound of Thunder," society has conquered time travel. For a fee, hunters could travel back in time to a point in history when a previously researched dinosaur was just about to expire so they could kill the extinct game. The time travelers stood upon a platform that hovered over the ancient ground, but they were ordered not to descend. One hunter does jump off the platform, however, and when the guides retrieve him and force him back to the platform, they note upon inspection that a butterfly lies crushed under the hunter's boot. They return to their present day to find in horror that everything has changed: a different language is spoken, and the democracy they left has been transformed into a totalitarian state.

Discussion about this short story would lead to the tenet. How could so much be changed by a circumstance so seemingly insignificant? The lesson became much more evident the year a student died in an alcohol-related car crash. The consequences radiated out to his friends and family and beyond—the wife that student never loved, the children he never created, the accomplishments left for others.

One year at the high school where I taught, my students and I researched alumni killed in battle to create a school memorial. The research brought us to Department of Defense records, amazingly detailed for victims of the Vietnam War, decreasingly so for Korea and the World Wars. A list of war casualties from the town newspapers brought our research group to the school vault to verify whether these deceased veterans were students who had attended our school.

We found that in the 1920s and 1930s student transcripts included photographs. My students were struck by the photos—the seemingly tough guy poses that served as a thin veil to adolescence.

They noted that honors students didn't seem to go to war. They noted that had those tough guys survived, their children might have been friends and classmates. They spoke about how those now dead must have wandered the same old hallways of our school, slamming the lockers with the same gusto on Fridays. They became reverential about these veterans, spoke about how their last moments must have been spent in pain, away from home and family. The lesson of what one poet called "the iron circumstance" burnt with those students of mine that week, and the tenet from which the lesson was crafted remains a pivotal understanding of life to me.

As a teacher, your responsibility for your actions is even keener. You must say and you must do up there, and what you say and do has profound implications, so profound that the meeker among us may just want to stand up there mute. You must say and you must do, however, for lives are in the balance. Think on that when you drag yourself into the building on a Monday morning, wishing to just shove worksheets in front of them for the day.

TENET: WE ARE PART OF A LEGACY

Very few of the students I have met can go far in this family-tree exercise. See how far you can go. For most of us, our memories peter out around the great-grandparent stage, even though those people, about whom we know little or nothing, carried our DNA strands and probably looked like us as well.

If any one of those on the diagram had a different fate, never had children or a spouse, you know the obvious consequence: no them, no you. One can surmise that they participated in a legacy of love and hope, that they loved their partner for a time, and hoped their offspring would have a better life. In Thornton Wilder's play *Our Town* such a theme is presented. The narrator admits that all we know of the past is what may be on contracts or business records. But, he mused, people went home each night, smoke rose from the chimneys of homes, and the cycle of life continued unabated.

I believe this legacy of hope belongs to all our students. Even today, where our family trees have transplanted roots and hybrid limbs, students need to know that they can continue and strengthen their legacy. They can continue even if the circumstances of their family lives are not entirely happy.

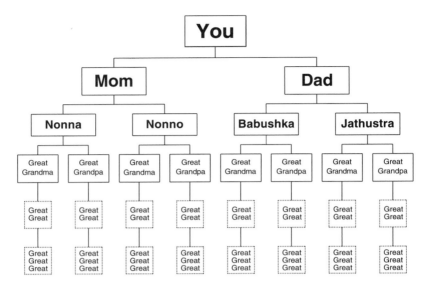

The possibility looms that life will present a family tree like this to any one of us:

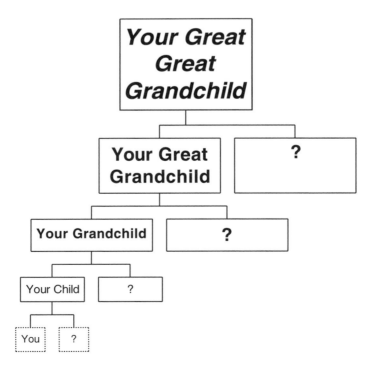

There will come a day when a great great grandchild of yours may know just as little about you as you did about the names that came before you and your mom and your dad. But your great great grandchild may hope as you did that there was a legacy of love involved, that a partner was loved for a time, and that there was hope for a child who might face a better life.

By such reflections are students shown that they are a part of something positive and life-long. That is the teacher's legacy. In a world of broken promises and fractured families, we teachers can give our students the possibility that they will find the happiness and solace all of us seek.

But remember that balance is the key. You must love your students but you must do so without taint. You cannot bring them home, nor have them as a part of your own life. You must realize the innate sadness (and ironically the best quality) of the teaching profession: you are in the business of saying goodbye. It is essential for them to move on to other circumstances that will help them prosper. It is a blessing that you will leave them after a time and turn to a new group with renewed wisdom, having learned from your errors with the previous group.

After a career of teaching high school seniors, I looked forward to the end of the high school year: the nostalgia of spring, the baleful "senior stare," the inevitable distraction of signing yearbooks and saying goodbye. If you work as hard as you can to reach and inspire your students, it will not be easy to remove yourself from their lives. But that is the way it works, and so you do it with grace and a smile.

A few graduates may continue correspondence with you, but for the most part, two return trips usually does it for an alumnus. The first time they return is to show off their new hair style or facial hair or pierced adornment. The second visit brings to them a realization: how puny the place looks! The teachers are focused on their current students, and the returning students discover that what they seek— what helped them during their years in the building—resides within themselves and not within the building. So part of their growing up is putting behind that which made them young, including you. As their teacher, you must learn to accept that and you must help them accept that.

TENET: DELAY JUDGMENT

If I can impress only one thing that will help you become effective teachers, it will be always remember to delay judgment. The majority of teaching errors result from disregarding this tenet. Teachers judge incorrectly all the time.

Scene: Student comes in without homework. But we want students to regard the homework we assign as important. We also want our students not to take advantage of us. So we lose patience. We lecture in front of all: "Homework is due when it's due. No exceptions." Fine. Wonderful. Order restored. Meanwhile, you discover later on that the student has spent the night in the emergency room with an ailing parent or has an otherwise legitimate circumstance. And you have lost the chance to acquire an ally. But your mania for an orderly atmosphere has certainly been enunciated. Bravo.

Students mask. What appears to be boredom is not, what appears to be disregard often is a cover for something else underlying. You cannot allow disrespectful behavior. But responding to a circumstance or a response or a vibe from a student in a thoughtless manner will often lead you to an incorrect assumption.

Delaying judgment will test you in class. The student who answers you in a manner you regard as disrespectful may not mean that you are the circumstance that disturbs the student. To elevate a student's level of upset because your notion of classroom demeanor is unbending may cause you to worsen the situation. Calm response is difficult in these circumstances, but it is necessary. And you can practice avoiding judgment while you gather more evidence. You can ask a second question in a lower voice. You can ask if the student wishes to be excused to collect his or her thoughts. You can ask the student to step outside the classroom for a moment so you can have a brief and private exchange. You can delay judging until you have an accurate perception on how to proceed.

Scene: You encounter a student you believe may have plagiarized. In this case, attacking without a judgment delay always brings out heated denial. Whenever I had a premonition about plagiarism, I learned to call the student in during conference hour to talk about the paper. I asked the student how he or she arrived at the interpretations in the submitted paper. After a few sentences, the student who had plagiarized invariably stumbled. But in most cases, I discovered that students had not yet learned the necessity of citing their sources. They needed to learn how to blend their personal perceptions with published ideas in a manner that reflects intellectual honesty.

As a teacher you can gauge by the conversation how brazen or how innocent the appropriation was, then decide on a course of corrective action. Haranguing a student right from the start of the conversation may make you feel like the Righteous Angel of Intellectual Honesty, but you do not make the circumstance a learning experience by pouring on vehemence. In fact, instructors who speak with vehemence about students, whether individually or by group, have settled into a spasm of judgment that prevents them from truly seeing their students. It reduces their potential for success.

If you hear yourself say "These kids can't . . . ," always remember that translates to "*I* can't . . . ," and that is the opening phrase of your limiting your competence through inappropriate judgment.

TENET: NEVER MAKE AN EXHAUSTED DECISION

This is the advice our parents gave us about important decisions like buying a home or choosing a spouse. It is equally important in the teaching profession. Heed this carefully: Your measurement as a teacher will not be gauged by how well you do with the students who adore you. Anyone can benefit from interacting with such students. But the student who gets on your nerves, the dislikable student, the one who smells, the one who knows how to irritate you, the whining student, the argumentative student—your response to these students will determine your effectiveness as a teacher.

You will not even get the chance to gauge how successful you are with such a student on a good day, when the sun shines and the birds twerp. No, it will be when you have everything going south, your relationship awry, your parents ailing, your teeth hurting, the interruptions ceaseless, the day endless and unsuccessful—on that day, when that unpleasant student approaches you, will be your defining moment.

A cross-country coach I know liked to say his team was as strong as his weakest runner. So you are as strong as you are on your weakest day. If you decide to judge that student during that moment without thoughtful reflection, you'll discover your own limitations. Hard lesson brought this realization to me. Here is the story:

In my heyday as a teacher, it was five shows daily and I was having a ball. I was good and I knew I was good. We laughed and learned and I was full of myself. Students were conniving to get into my classes, and I accepted them because it was all part of the merry express. Show time in the suburbs!

Such large classes gave me reams of papers to read, and I tore into them with relish sitting on the floor by the TV watching whatever. Some nights I would plop asleep right atop them. On one of those nights I remember reading the first paragraph of a paper I assigned. I did not like how the first paragraph was structured. In those years I was obsessive about first paragraphs: "Your first paragraphs are the map of the territory of the rest of your paper!" I would literally shout to the students. "Show an intriguing map and your reader will follow into the territory of your paper."

This student's first paragraph wasn't going anywhere, and it was late. I circled the first paragraph, didn't read the rest, and jotted a note on the cover page asking the student to come see me for a conference. Then a few days later a student came to me with a transfer form. In the early parts of a term students transfer in and out for all sorts of reasons—schedule changes in other classes, a desire to get out earlier for work opportunities. Since my classes were overcrowded anyway, I signed the note, wished the student well, and returned to teaching. Five shows daily! Show time in the suburbs!

November came—time for parent-teacher conferences. In my heady heyday I loved conference night. Other teachers dreaded that evening, but I reveled in the love fest: "You are such a wonderful teacher!" moms and dads would exclaim. "If I could be as good a parent as you, I would be grateful!" I exclaimed back. "You're great!" "You're great too!" Air kisses abounded. Affirmation overload.

But the last appointment I had that evening was a name I did not recognize. No matter, thought I, it could be a remarriage, or a parent road testing me for their child's appearance in my class the following year. A stocky gentleman in a mustache quietly sat down and looked at me.

"Do you remember _____," he asked me in a quiet voice.

"Uh, yes, I believe he was in my class for a short time." Quick look in my grade book. "Yes, for a week or so."

"Do you remember assigning him a paper?"

Another glance at my book. "Uh, yes I see he was here for the first paper assignment I gave, but he dropped my class before a grade was recorded."

"Do you remember reading his paper?" He hadn't moved at all, just intently looking at me.

"Uh, I don't really recall. I read so many papers."

He handed me the paper. "Will you read it now?"

You know those moments in your career when the hairs on your neck fling up and corticotrophin, that substance that filters down your spinal column when you are frightened, begins its descent. Those are the moments when you know you are in the deep end, and I hope you never have too many of those moments, for the world really whirls and the bottom really drops.

So there was the first paragraph I had circled two months prior while exhausted in front of my TV watching whatever. This time I read the entire paper. And what I read was remarkably like the story line of Judith Guest's great novel *Ordinary People*. This young man wrote of his brother's death and his inability to accept it, his struggle with blaming himself for causing that death, his shame at having to live on while his parents wrestled with the loss of their more favored son. It was truly a remarkable reflection.

I forced myself to look up at this father, still not moving, now with tears running down his face. "My son has been in therapy since his brother's death. He has never been able to fully express how he felt—to his therapist, to us, no one." He now slowed to articulate each word. "This paper was the first time he put his complete thoughts into writing," he said, his voice rising, "and *this is how you responded to it?*"

What could be said? "Sorry . . . I was tired . . . Sorry."

The father got up and left to relate his tale to the principal. And that was the year I won the Golden Apple Award for Excellence in Teaching. Five shows daily. Show time in the suburbs.

On that evening all that hubris dissolved away. My lost opportunity weighed on me for weeks afterward. Fortunately for me, there was a positive resolution to this incident. I was allowed into the home of this family who received and accepted my abject apology. I championed the young man for bringing himself on the road to healing with no comfort or assistance provided by me to whom he had entrusted his pain. The father shook my hand as I left, but his eyes were unforgiving, and I thank him to this day for that lesson.

Like many teachers, I have a large envelope somewhere in my possession with all the nice things written to me by students and parents tucked inside it. I never throw away such words, although I never really reread them either. I daresay you may have such an envelope as well. On the front of my envelope, I have stapled the paper from the student who reached out to me whom I turned away in my blind and arrogant ignorance. Each time I file away another word of thanks or appreciation, that stapled paper reminds me that for every moment with every student I must never again make a decision based on distraction or exhaustion.

TENET: WE TEACH WHAT WE ARE FAR MORE THAN WE TEACH WHAT WE TEACH

Your very approach manifests what you are, what you value, and what you believe. The obverse is also true: If you reflect on nothing and stand for nothing and value nothing, then the vapid quality of your lessons will exhibit emptiness. A novice teacher may not know a plethora of instructional techniques, may not have strong subject matter grasp, may not have a handle on understanding children. But all these can be developed if one has a set of tenets that define the reasons you wish to teach.

Remember your own favorite teacher. His or her lessons are only dimly recalled now, and the quizzes and tests are long forgotten. But you do recall the essence of that person. That excellent teacher's kindness, or way of boosting your desire to learn, is what you recollect. You retain what that teacher was to you. You may teach subject, but mostly you teach what you are, the way you animate the subject. Your essence is the contribution you make to the education of the children in your charge.

Bill Ayers, university scholar and distinguished professor in the College of Education at the University of Illinois at Chicago, is most eloquent and succinct on this point. Bill has long argued that the key to success in teaching is becoming a student of your students. The more you learn about them, the more you are able to intuit from careful observation and reflection on their words and actions who they are and why they are who they are. In their words and in their silences are the keys to understanding them. In their posture and in their manner are the cues you must learn to note. Try not to overlook possibilities that your students are communicating with you.

So too the underlying dynamic of the classroom offers your students the opportunity to observe you to gauge your effectiveness. They will watch your demeanor. They will tune in to signs of nervousness, of false bravado, of underlying personal problems affecting your mien. Your students may wildly misjudge how old you are, but they will be uncanny in their ability to perceive whether you are worthy of their attention and respect.

When you were a student, how long did it take you to size up your teachers? Can you recall, perhaps with some embarrassment, a time when you and your fellow students went for the jugular on a teacher you disdained? What were the cues in that teacher's behavior that turned you from giving the person a chance to dismissive behavior? Did that teacher have a fumbling style, play favorites, tend toward anger, show bias in word or deed? Whether subtle or obvious, that teacher's essence was communicated to you as a student. And if you as a teacher are not properly prepared with your own tenets, with the underlying set of principles that bring you in front of your own students, then your weaknesses will be evident regardless of the camouflage you don.

TENET: IN WHAT SEEMS THE MOST INSIGNIFICANT IS OFTEN THE MOST IMPORTANT

You will be continually surprised in your teaching at how the simplest of gestures and the most casual of circumstances can have the most profound effect on your students.

You may believe in the grand gesture and the dramatic pronouncements—I sure do. I wanted my classes to be anthems. I wanted to lead classes that had the same impact as Bruce Springsteen's early songs: powerful, complete, emotional, overwhelming. It was in my later years that I discovered that the truly important and effective teachable moments were quieter: the encouragement written in the margin of a journal, or the offhand remark that brightened a student's dour day. After years of practice, you become attuned to the possibility of such instances—teachable moments as they are commonly called, where the possibility exists that you can by decision or word choice profoundly change a student's opinion about himself or herself.

New teachers often miss these moments because they are focused so narrowly and so widely at the same time. New teachers worry about time, about following a lesson plan, about asking the prewritten questions, about whether or when the high-maintenance student will kick into need overdrive, all while the teachable moments pass without notice. And the trouble with traditional teacher preparation is that little attention is given to the perception of student cues in verbal and nonverbal communication. Anger, hope, doubt, disbelief, concern, apathy, arrogance—the entire array of adolescent human emotion can be seen in your classroom as in those Magic Eye pictures you have to stare at to see the hidden eagle or mountain range.

But if you enter the classroom with your own set of teaching tenets, then you will know where to look and what to do when you see the next teachable moment. If, for example, one of your tenets is "All students shall feel empowered in my class," then you will note signs of student apprehension as soon as they occur and you will be able to respond to them before they escalate. It's a bit like researching before buying a certain model car and suddenly seeing similar models on the road everywhere you drive. Having your own set of teaching tenets attunes your eye to what your students are emanating.

Make crafting your tenets your first priority. From your tenets will emerge the frame of your class, allowing you to create units that support and reveal the frame, allowing lessons to follow that will vivify those units. Having no tenets, struggle will ensue.

REFLECTIVE EXERCISES

1. Your Legacy

With today's technology, we have advantages our ancestors did not. We can record our image, our words, our thoughts. Record yours: What would you say to your future children's children yet unborn? What would you wish to hear them say to you?

2. Your Teaching Tenets

Revisit the statement you created at the end of Chapter 2 about the one thing always true in your classroom. Try placing that statement at the top of your list of teaching tenets. What other tenets should you have? Allow this list to keep expanding as you continue in this profession.

CHAPTER SEVEN

Classroom Ethics

68 What-Ifs That Will
Make Any Teacher Say "Yikes!"

How long do you think it will take for this kind of moment to happen to you: a circumstance will occur in your classroom or in the school or in the cafeteria or faculty lounge, and you will pause a moment and think to yourself, "You know, college never prepared me for handling this!"

You will exit your traditional teacher preparation program at the fine University of Wherever with their good wishes, but unless the place is extraordinary in its devotion to aftercare, you will receive scant assistance or mentoring thereafter. You will arrive with your mile-wide, inch-deep command of subject matter, your limited knowledge of children, and your still incomplete knowledge of yourself. The series of maps carefully constructed in your mind and heart will now enter the territory of your own classroom.

Finally, you have your walls (if you're lucky enough not to share rooms), your grade book, your children, and your responsibility to heal or harm or do nothing. Then you begin, and within seconds of beginning, I daresay, you will come across a moment that you have

Acknowledgments: The author thanks Peg Cain for permission to use her "what if" game in this chapter. The author also thanks David Ripley for permission to use the situations he crafted for ethics discussion in his School Law course.

not prepared yourself to encounter. For most new teachers, these are not usually "A-ha!" moments of sudden discovery. These are likelier to be moments that elicit a "Yikes!" or a "WHAT?" or almost certainly a "HELP!"

Every teacher who has passed through the traditional pathway has tales of the chasm that exists between the experiences of traditional preparation and the real-life responsibilities of the teaching profession. I recall with the nostalgia only experience can provide my first English department chairman. He was a courtly and deeply decent man, who gave me in July the textbooks I needed to review for my first year's teaching assignment. All summer long, I studied those textbooks and planned the dickens out of how I would approach the first unit, writing down my questions for the lessons to come on the backs of business-size envelopes. On my first day I discovered that my colleague had given me the wrong texts. What he had described as a remedial class was in fact a college-bound one, and vice versa. I could hear in my mind Clint Eastwood in the movie *Heartbreak Ridge* shouting, "You're a Marine: you adapt, you improvise, and you overcome." Well, I was no Marine, and at the time it seemed likelier that my teacher preparation had been a prelude to my true career in improvisational comedy.

During my very first week of teaching, a young girl came up to me to ask if she could go to the bathroom. As she asked, her thumb slipped under one of the buttons of her blouse and flicked the button into my face. Before I could respond to that surprise, the young girl collapsed into a seizure in front of me. I had never seen a seizure before. I had no idea what to do. My first impulse was to clear the classroom. Why? I had no idea. "Everyone get out of here!" I shouted. The students were happy to oblige, and in an instant 24 young people under my responsibility were out roaming the halls.

My second impulse was to try to pick the girl up and carry her to the nurse's office. Have you ever contended with the strength of someone in seizure? She quickly swatted me aside. I was grateful that a colleague wondering why students were wandering the halls poked her head in, grasped the situation, and pressed the call button. Call button? What's that, I wondered?

That moment, one of my very first as a professional educator, clearly showed that my college had helped prepare me to do a fine job explaining how a poem worked but had offered me nothing at all on what to do when a student convulsed. And at that moment, knowing about convulsions was much more important to me than poetry.

Twelve Classroom Situations

Welcome to the learning curve! Perhaps as student teachers or as novice teachers you noticed that you were in a double bind. You didn't know the material coming in, yet you still had to prepare a lesson to impart what you yourself had barely learned. So how could you notice, let alone act upon, the multiple cues, teachable moments, and subtextual messages your students were sending with their questions or their body language or their silence? And where would you find the resources to respond when a moment came up that had no reference to the lesson plan at hand or to literature, science, or any college course or law school course you'd ever taken?

The bulk of teaching occurs in the multitude of decisions you will make in reaction to circumstances you had not anticipated encountering. Those decisions, the ones you are forced to make when you are unsure, distracted, or overburdened, will determine the quality of your teaching, just as the measure of your teaching will derive not from the students who love you but from the ones who most challenge. This is why operating under a set of tenets will help you, because when situations arise causing you to enter a "yikes" moment, your principles will be there to guide you.

What makes these situations so vexing is that they're often not curricular. When I visited methodology classes with prospective teachers, they bombarded me with "What do you do when" questions. Those new teachers didn't want to talk about how Madeline Hunter had transformed instructional practice. They wanted to talk about the young Maddie Hunters in their classrooms, the students who were providing those extracurricular "yikes" moments. Those moments arise not only when working with your students, but also with their parents, with administrators, with colleagues, with the central office, with board members. The new teacher is often exhausted for very good reason.

A systematic approach to these untoward situations would take up an entire text in and of itself. If you are lucky, the veteran teacher who befriends and mentors you will also give you instruction in the culture of your school community, allowing you to laugh with him or her in the recounting of errors made and life lessons learned. The following scenarios are memorable ones for me because they happened during my teaching career, when I erred as often as I chose correctly in the decisions I made. Perhaps they can serve as preamble to one of the great challenges you will encounter in your teaching career: teaching-situation ethics.

> 1. A student writes in a journal or essay perspectives that could be construed as suicidal. Or a student confides in you that he or she has considered suicide. You are the only person this student has told about these feelings. The student pleads with you to keep the conversations confidential, because the student fears shame, anger, or recrimination that would be too much to bear if you divulge the problem to others.

We so focus on student feelings today that this scenario should offer no challenge to you, but as a young teacher it vexed me considerably. In my "I can change the world one person at a time" stage, I kept the confidence of a disturbed student, to my deep distress. The result was one evening I received a phone call at home from this student, who had slashed her wrists and was calling in a dim haze from a phone booth. She described nearby landmarks, allowing me to visualize where she was, and there I went in my car on a Saturday night, to bring a bleeding and disoriented student to my home, where my wife and I bandaged her. Whatever was I thinking?

In a subsequent call to her therapist, he made it very clear that I the unwitting fool was not helping her in the least. Still I was surprised when this student's next act was to tape a suicide note to my front door. I recall the absolute frustration of being so out of my league, so thoroughly exhausted by the mental anguish of working with her sadness, that for a moment I thought to myself, "All right, die then!" as I read her taped note. But then I went in and called the police. Fortunately she was found before tragedy occurred, she received the help she needed, and she recovered and moved on with her life.

That's the amazing thing sometimes. If a professional can intervene in time with students who can't see through their unhappy today to the promise of tomorrow, odds are those students will recover well.

If such an event happens to you, tell everyone! Make copies and distribute them to counselor, principal, psychologist, and department chair. Law now forces our hand, making teachers liable if such steps are not heeded. Allow those trained in such matters to assist. The child may very well be giving you permission to tell everyone by telling you. Risking losing someone's trust is worth the effort. It is far better to lose that trust than to stare at that child's casket searching your memory for cues about what you might have done better or faster. In this circumstance, you act upon the principle that you are not an island, nor are you the only person on the earth who can help someone. That lone rebel image of the teacher portrayed by Robin Williams in *Dead Poet's Society* is dangerous. When you start to think you are the only person in the building who really cares about your students, you will start to err.

> 2. You notice a student of yours with whom you are on good terms in close physical contact with another student of the same gender. In the teacher's lounge, some of your colleagues comment about having witnessed such activity. What if anything do you do?

Here, your own moral code may conflict with your good sense and place you in a position to err. The problem surfaces when you do not delay judgment. Remember that what seems is often not what is. Further, what right do you have to pass judgment over the sexual proclivities of your students, unless those students' activities are marring the educational climate of your room?

In this circumstance, a well-intentioned colleague felt honor bound to pull one of the students in this scenario aside to warn her that her reputation could be harmed if she engaged in this kind of immoral activity. This student immediately came to interrupt a meeting I was having with a colleague to tearfully demand to know if any more of our colleagues were discussing her moral stature. This was followed next day by a meeting with the student and her attorney father, broadly intimating that this teacher's words were "actionable," a phrase I hope you never have to hear in your career.

What a mess! This entire trauma originated from a decision to make a moralistic judgment based on inference. While exceedingly valuable to use in developing our insight and sensitivity, relying on inference rather than knowledge to make judgments can lead us astray. In the realm of students' interpersonal relationships, our perceptions often are the victims of our incomplete knowledge. But the overriding question to ask yourself is what business is it of yours to comment on your students' sexuality?

Consider how you would respond to this similar scenario.

3. A student confides in you that he or she believes she is not heterosexual, but isn't sure, and seeks your advice.

This scenario has all the markings of "They never told me how to handle this in college." You may have gained the trust and respect of a student who seeks words from you on a subject you may find personally immoral if not distasteful. Now you certainly can brush the student off by claiming you don't talk about personal matters, and that will clear your responsibility from further concern. But do your instincts lead you to such a callous response? Do you want to pontificate, quote Biblical passages and warn the student of the damnation to come from wandering away from sexual orthodoxy? Well, that might assuage your sense of righteousness, but do you see yourself engaging in such dogmatism? But are you also uncomfortable embracing homosexuality or encouraging further experimentation? Do you see yourself as a proselytizer for alternative lifestyles?

Any way you go, this one is a difficult call. Why do you think a student might confide such a thing to you? What would that student be hoping for from you? If you think *acceptance,* you may have something. The student may be struggling with a matter that requires intense personal reflection. If that student has high regard for you, losing that regard would be harmful. Maybe the best thing you could tell that student is that your own regard for people does not center on a personal matter such as sexual orientation.

You can admit that you admire this student; you will continue to admire this student. I have always contended that the most silent minority in the school setting, the most isolated and the most aggrieved, is the gay high school student. You may not wish to advance the gay lifestyle, and that is fine, but you need not harangue against it either.

How many students do you think teachers have lost because we did not offer understanding and acceptance of the students' true selves, regardless of the challenges confronting them? Why would any one of us want to continue any young person's pain?

In such cases, it does matter if you accept your students and they sense your acceptance. The price of your regard should not be their adherence to your own version of morality and righteousness.

4. A student asks your advice on where to obtain an abortion.

Would your response depend on your own opinion about abortion? Should you give in to the temptation to launch into a pro-life or pro-choice diatribe? Should you give this student the advice requested? What might happen if the student followed your advice—say obtained an abortion at a place you recommended and then discovered it was against the opinion of her parents who were now looking to you for redress of their grievance? What if you counseled a student to keep a child against the wishes of her family? Is it your place to offer such advice, or is it more appropriate to serve as a resource directing her to the person(s) who are more appropriate to offer such advice?

This is one of those circumstances when you must realize that you are part of a larger educational community devoted to helping all of the children in that community. This student may have come to you because she trusts you, but that does not mean this student should trust only you. As part of an educational community, you are still helping your students even if you ask for help. The teacher who is a lone wolf may look romantic, but that kind of romance is high risk.

5. A student asks if you have and can offer (a) a breath mint, (b) a pain reliever (aspirin, ibuprofen), (c) a feminine napkin/tampon.

Most of us will rightfully see the dangers inherent in giving students any kind of medication, not knowing if the student has allergies or other conditions that could be aggravated by that medication. Breath mints may be relatively harmless, but there are some schools that will advise you never to offer anyone anything, while other schools have classrooms stocked with tissue boxes and other supplies free and open for students to use. When a student during summer school asked me if I had any tampons, she clearly was a student in distress. I directed her to my colleague next door for assistance. Let your conscience be your guide in matters of what you offer students, but always be wary of offering anything medicinal.

6. A student walks in to your classroom complaining bitterly about the poor teaching ability of another teacher. This is not the first time you have heard complaints about this teacher. You also may not hold him or her in particular regard. The student then asks your opinion about this teacher.

So, ye who believe in truth at all times, how do you respond here? Do you agree with the student, allowing yourself to be known as the teacher who criticizes colleagues in front of students? Do you disagree with the student, thereby offering tacit approval of instructional competence that you do in fact find lacking? Do you say nothing?

Here you must tread with care. A student's disapproval of a teacher may be based on many factors, ranging from resentment about a single homework assignment to a long series of truly stultifying classes. At issue here is whether you believe you need to keep peace in the faculty lounge by keeping quiet when students complain about colleagues or whether you take it upon yourself to join your disapproval with theirs. What advantage do you gain by agreeing with them? What might you lose? Are you thinking value in discretion here? Quite so! However, compare that scenario to this one:

7. A student confides in you that another teacher has made inappropriate comments or has made the student feel uncomfortable by his or her actions, gestures, looks, or words.

This is altogether different. Sexual harassment policy established by schools mandates a response. Here you must advocate for the student, abide by the established policy, and speak with the immediate supervisor of the teacher involved.

A student once told me that a teacher made her feel uncomfortable by asking all the students to stand on their desks. As she was wearing a short skirt that day, the request made her feel funny, since she connected it with a vague feeling of unease she had long felt around this instructor. Was this harassment? Could this have been a misconstruction of an unusual classroom activity? It is not up to you to make such distinctions. The student feels unease, and you must report that unease to a supervisor. The supervisor is responsible for determining such distinctions and for mentoring (or, if appropriate, warning) the teacher in question. There will always be gradations in circumstances that could allow you to respond differently. The teacher must be savvy enough to recognize the proper response when those circumstances occur and be ready to make a decision, often in a matter of seconds.

8. You notice one of your students has his/her pants zipper undone.

You may think that teacher preparation is about readying yourself for the responsibility of bringing knowledge's light to a world darkened by ignorance, but I must tell you that in all my years of preparing teachers, the zipper question is the most common "what if" question asked. What is it about zippers that make us all frenzied? What threat to universal order exists here?

Philosophy aside, the question persists. How do you draw the attention of such a student and avoid drawing other students' attention at the same time? Let's assume the solution is not to shout it out so everyone can hear, or to whisper directly into the student's ear while the rest of the class is watching you and then the student's quick and embarrassed reaction.

Try a misdirection method instead. Direct the students' attention to the far side of the classroom while at the same time leaning over and whispering to the student in question. I warrant this will work with zippers undone or buttons undone or with visible snot or even with a fabric softener sheet poking out of a shirtsleeve (my own personal embarrassing moment). Crisis resolved, humiliation averted, the world can continue turning, and you can proceed with your mission.

9. A student expresses his or her love to you in a letter.

While you retain youth and energy, students will be drawn to that youthful energy. Some will translate that attraction into the crushes so common in school life. Face it, you are young and some of your students will develop a crush on you. This unnerves the new teacher, and here one must respond with sensitivity and absolute clarity. Do not mince words, but do not belittle. Do not worry about hurtful feelings and do not be anything but clear. Do not express thanks or appreciation for such words, for that may unintentionally encourage a student. Somewhere in your words there must be a clear message that says, "I am not here for that purpose for you."

In today's litigious society, you must be clear and forthright. You may experience deep feelings for your students, but the essential fact of the matter is that you are only a temporary presence in their lives, dedicated to assisting them to learn more and to feel better about themselves and their own worth and purpose in life. Then they will move on and you will move on. You cannot be anything else to them. You cannot take them home, cannot keep them with you, cannot witness their progress through the stages of life, cannot be a forever presence with them. Students may see you as a sounding board for their own attractiveness, and they may flirt innocently. You as teacher must recognize the ephemeral and unsubstantial nature of that flirtation and make no indication of acceptance or encouragement.

10. A student asks you to drive him/her home.

More situation challenges exist in the realm of the extracurricular than in the classroom. New teachers are expected to advise clubs, and in the club context a teacher is more at ease with students, prompting circumstances that could blur the teacher-student distinction.

In this scenario different schools have different policies. Some schools may forbid transporting students in personal vehicles for safety reasons, while others may provide insurance riders that protect the teacher-driver under the policy of the school. You want the students to arrive home safely, but given the potential liability involved, you must be prudent. You want to avoid being in your car with one student, especially if that student is not of your gender. I advise against transporting students in your car altogether.

11. Two students begin to fight in your classroom.

This scenario is fraught with circumstantial elements. The age of the students and the volatility of their confrontation must be gauged. Your responsibility is for their safety, and you will have reflected before you begin work on what role you will play when a fight occurs. Even with that reflection, you may find yourself making a snap decision, and perhaps it will need to be different from the one you planned.

What has worked for me in fight situations is an understanding of fight protocol. Usually, one person is more aggressive or aggrieved than the other, who acts in a reactive rather than a proactive role. I probably would move quickly to the more aggressive of the two, thinking that the less aggressive combatant would be relieved about my interference and not try to sucker punch over my back. I would stand with legs apart and bottom of both palms against the attacker, repeating variations of "you don't want to do this." Maneuvering the more aggressive person toward the classroom door would be my path.

The circumstance of violence in schools usually occurs without warning, triggered by events in the "other discipline" of the school halls. It presents you with a real challenge. How will you respond? Will you yell out in an attempt to get help? Will you intervene? Will you flee? You really will not know until it occurs, and when you respond you will respond based on your instincts. One thing is for sure, you will not respond based upon a careful reconsideration of this discussion or any other you may have had in your traditional teacher preparation courses. But you must and will respond, and in that response you will learn something about yourself unrevealed in your professional preparation.

Sometimes, when the aggressor is stronger, you gain only time in which to get help. If the aggressor carries a weapon of any kind, you are in a different and difficult circumstance, one where advice does not come easily.

Once I entered school in the morning right at the start of an imbroglio. I moved instinctively to the aggressor, a behemoth footballer. While preventing his forward movement, we tumbled to the ground. I lay across his waist, staring at his feet. "Just don't move," I said. He was motionless and twice my size. I was just starting to congratulate myself on my effect on behemoths when I turned my head to see my colleague, who had lost his hand as a youth, kneeling alongside the student, his hook hovering, saying simply "Stay." So much for my advice! The simple truth is there is no handbook for these circumstances. What you will do will be determined not by preparation, but by instinct. Still, you must prepare to witness and respond. But what about the moment you truly cannot foresee:

12. A student brandishes a weapon in your class.

Only once in my career did I disarm a student who brought a Bowie knife to class mainly to show off. I asked for it, he refused, dared me to take it from him. I did, using a simple and simply lucky gesture I learned in a martial arts class I took years before. But his stance was not threatening, nor his hold on the knife accurate enough to cause harm. I remanded him to the deans and trembled for the rest of the day.

I don't have an answer for this scenario. As I tell prospective teachers, my job is to protect students. Yet, I also want very much to live to walk my daughter down the aisle at her wedding and to watch my son grow to manhood and to take my wife with me to my dotage. I frankly do not know if I would use my body to shield a student from harm or use a student to shield me from harm. You would think such thoughts would never need to surface in this line of work. But we all know today that the unthinkable does occur, and what we do under unthinkable circumstances remains a personal decision. Like police officers and fire fighters, teachers today may work in hazardous settings. It is our duty to protect as well as instruct their children.

But consider the complexity of protecting the children in your classroom. One of the prospective teachers I worked with was observing in an elementary class when the mother of one of the students entered the room. Enraged that her child had damaged a textbook and that the school had fined her, the mother ran to her child and began beating him. The teacher directed the other children to move away from the mother and her child, but allowed her to continue to harm her child. At one point the child broke free and ran to huddle behind the legs of the student teacher, who stood frozen in fear. The mother finally dragged her child from the room.

What would you have done in this circumstance? Is your room a place where violence is never tolerated, where you will do whatever necessary to protect your children? What if that means preventing parents from doing in your room what they may be doing at home? Or do you allow a parent the right to discipline a child, even if the other children witness an upsetting display of adult aggression? The situation happened just that fast, and the teacher responded instantly, albeit incorrectly in the eyes of the school district, which disciplined her for not intervening. The harrowing point is that the courses you are taking to prepare you to teach may not touch anywhere near this subject. They may, to use a metaphor I have used before, discuss John Dewey, but they will not prepare you to deal with Mrs. Dewey when she is beating up on Johnny in your classroom because she had to pay a fine.

This is why the late Dave Sanders of Columbine High School is a hero. Shot while directing students to a room away from his murderer, he acted as a human entrusted with the care of other humans. No one taught him what to do if someone began shooting at his students. No class in self-defense brought him any enlightenment. He acted as he would have had he been in any other profession. Sobering thoughts as you prepare to enter a world you and I hope will be full of paper-mâché, giggling, and easily resolved adolescent angst.

EXPECTING THE UNEXPECTED

Rushworth Kidder (1996) has written extensively and well on the situation ethics faced by teachers. His work at the Institute for Global Ethics focuses on four major patterns that apply to nearly all unexpected situations that can occur in teaching:

1. Individual versus community, when the needs of the individual conflict with the needs of a group.

2. Truth versus honesty, when the integrity of an individual is at odds with that individual's responsibility.

3. Short-term versus long-term, when the needs of the moment clash with deferred needs.

4. Justice versus mercy, when fairness is in conflict with compassion.

Kidder's work on this subject merits your close attention as you attempt to prepare for situations you cannot predict—the unexpected that requires immediate response. Here are scenarios prepared by my colleague and friend Dave Ripley for prospective teachers. How would you respond?

1. You are a high school women's basketball coach and one of your athletes tells you her stepfather has been physically abusing her. She begs you not to tell anyone, as she is afraid that the step-father will harm her mother or her younger sister.

2. You are a middle school teacher and a parent calls you, claiming that you called her son "stupid." What you did say, after the boy made an inappropriate comment in class, was that his point "was the stupidest thing you ever heard." You deny calling the boy "stupid" but sense that the parent will contact the principal if you do not apologize.

3. You are a new teacher in an upper middle-class suburban high school district. Several students ask your help in approaching the administration seeking permission to form a gay/lesbian student organization, which they would like you to sponsor.

4. You are a second-grade teacher and one of your students, an especially needy and insecure lad, has gotten into the habit of giving you a hug at the end of every day. A veteran teacher enters the room while this is taking place, seems surprised, but says nothing.

5. A fifth-grade student in your class has a learning disability in reading. She benefits greatly from taking her tests and quizzes with the resource teacher, who can read questions aloud and clarify terms, but the girl hates being "singled out" when she leaves the room. You

could probably support her more in class to her benefit, but at the expense of time and attention to your other students.

6. You are a high school coach having a successful season. The team has begun going out for pizza after each contest and they are eager to invite you. You note during conversations that the students have begun to regard you as one of the group. You enjoy the fellowship of these students but worry about blurring the lines between teacher and student.

Fascinating. The situation ethics of teaching approaches the complexity of chess and bridge—endless combinations of circumstances and participants that require you to make decisions, important decisions that will in part define your success as a teacher. But traditional professional preparation programs pay scant attention to this subject.

When I first began appearing as a guest speaker in university methodology classes, I was thunderstruck by the unending desire of prospective teachers for answers to "what if" questions. The gulf between the theoretician and the practitioner could not be wider than in this area, and the savvy new teacher will learn to acquire a support group and a mentor for help in considering these circumstances.

Sometimes the interaction of humans provides moments no educator could ever predict. One summer I was hired as a tutor for a young man recovering from major surgery. We developed a rapport that continued as the fall began, and he was assigned to my class. One day as he entered the classroom wearing a jacket, I noticed a piece of a plastic bag sticking out of his pocket. "Hey," I shouted to all present, "what have we here, your drug stash?" and I tugged at the plastic, suddenly producing a rather large bag filled with reefers. The moment froze like a scene in a Brueghel painting. The kids looked at me, the kid looked at me, I looked at the bag—the moment froze in time. Did I just do an illegal search and seizure? Could I keep the bag? Return the bag in a room full of witnesses? Help! Yikes! As it turned out, I confiscated the bag and reported the incident to the deans, receiving a modest rebuke for searching a student.

At the time, search and seizure laws on school grounds were vague. Currently, schools have the authority to conduct locker searches for contraband, though the extent of personal searches requires careful consideration, far more consideration than my action offered. While school lockers have been deemed to be not the sole property of students (*Zamora v Pomeroy*, 639F 2d, 665), students must be given notice that their right to privacy is limited. The case of *State of New Jersey v Moore* (1992) allows searches of book bags, pockets, or purses, but the reason for the search must be expressed and the search must end if it reveals no prohibited items. *The National Association of Attorneys General School Search Reference Guide of 1999* states that "the right of freedom of movement enjoyed by school age children is far more limited than the right of liberty enjoyed by adult citizens. . . . Schools may impose significant restrictions . . . also on their ability to use and possess personal property." The U.S. Supreme Court in the case of *New Jersey v T.L.O.* recognized that "the preservation of order and of a proper educational environment requires close supervision of children."

The net result of these decisions is that while students do possess the rights to privacy of person as guaranteed by the Fourth Amendment to the U.S. Constitution, those rights are balanced by a school's responsibility to protect its students. Therefore school officials and teachers can conduct searches when they have a reason to suspect a school law has been or will be violated, or if students are in danger. The law even specifies when searches of person are in order.

About this time you may be wondering why this discussion is so far afield from field trips and jack-o'-lanterns on bulletin boards and apples on the big desk. Teaching situations are so varied and compelling in their complexity! Your response to scenarios you never thought you would encounter will be more indicative of your effect than the grades you earned in your education courses.

PRACTICING FOR "WHAT IF"

My colleague Peg Cain approaches the subject of situation ethics in teaching with a set of cards dispensed in her classes with prospective teachers. You too can practice the "what if" game and seek advice from veteran teachers, even if only to provide a template by which to consider your own responses to what can occur in the amazing dynamic that is the American classroom.

What will you do when

1. A student calls you by your first name?

2. A student asks if you have ever taken hallucinogens?

3. A parent says you don't have enough experience to teach?

4. A student tells you "My mother is dying"?

5. A sixth-grader tells you she's pregnant?

6. A parent comes on to you?

7. A colleague details your mistakes at the faculty lunch table?

8. You notice a student crying in class?

9. A student says, "We learned this last year"?

10. A student says, "I'm dropping out as soon as I'm sixteen"?

11. A student calls another a "faggot"?

12. A student says to you, "Fuck you"?

13. A student says to you, "My mother's a slut"?

14. A student throws up?

15. A bee enters the classroom?

16. You feel an attraction to a student?

17. A student farts?

18. A student becomes the class victim?

19. A student says, "I was never good in (the subject you teach)"?

20. A student consistently smells bad?

21. A student faints?

22. You don't know the answer to a question?

23. A student asks, "Are you a virgin"?

24. A student says, "This is so stupid!"?

25. A student says, "I hate this school"?

26. A student asks, "When are we ever going to use this stuff in real life"?

27. A student says, "I turned my paper in—you must have lost it"?

28. A student reports another student is cheating?

29. A student plagiarizes?

30. A student says, "You're boring"?

31. A student says, "My dad says teachers are lazy because they only work 180 days a year"?

32. You see a weapon in someone's locker?

33. There's a mouse in the classroom?

34. A student asks, "Are you living with your boyfriend/ girlfriend"?

35. A student reports one of her classmates is sexually involved with a teacher?

36. You lose your grade book?

37. A student gives you an expensive Christmas present?

38. Money is missing from your desk?

39. You catch a boy and a girl, or two boys or two girls, half-naked in the janitor's closet?

40. A girl wears provocative clothing in the classroom, causing disruption?

41. A boy enters wearing a T-shirt with words on it you find offensive?

42. A student performs well on in-class assignments but never turns in homework?

43. A student is regularly absent on test day?

44. A student tells you she or he must take medication periodically throughout the day?

45. A student says, "I can't take this test. I have PMS"?

46. A student says, "This is my favorite class"?

47. A student looks at another student's paper during a test?

48. Your students will not follow directions?

49. Your students wander the room at will?

50. You cannot fight the urge to be angry or to cry?

More than a parlor game, these exercises will bring you to a critical understanding that your stature as a teacher will derive from more than the subject matter that you have learned to teach. You cannot underestimate the need for subject matter mastery, but there also is this other situational element of the profession that requires your quick and accurate decision. Let your tenets be your guide.

REFLECTIVE EXERCISE

Try to determine how you would respond to any of the 50 situations presented here. Compare yours to a colleague's decision. Then find a veteran teacher and compare both responses to the veteran's. Shouldn't there be an encyclopedia of these somewhere? Start crafting yours.

CHAPTER EIGHT

Major Stresses in the Teaching Profession

Why You Must Remain a Teacher

This chapter addresses frustration, not the kind engendered by your efforts or your students, but by the nature of the teaching profession and by some of those within it.

If you are reading this book, then you are striving to become an excellent teacher. You fear that the nation has too many teachers who do not strive for excellence and you have vowed you will not be one of them. You will put in hours untold perfecting your craft. Your personal life will be affected by your dedication. You will learn from your mistakes. But along the way you will also learn that there are some truths inherent in our profession that will infuriate you. This chapter focuses on two of those major stressors:

- The absence of a career ladder in our profession's definition of a teacher.
- The presence in our profession of colleagues who cannot or will not work to improve their craft, thereby degrading the title "teacher."

I focus on these aspects because as you acclimate to teaching during years two through five and begin to enlarge your view of our profession, these stressors will frustrate you.

You may be tempted to speak out, but you will also perceive that the teaching profession, like many others, has its own code of silence. You may be tempted to move toward an activist role in improving the standards of our profession, but you will also definitely feel the conformist's pull. A great number of teachers leave the profession after five years, and I hope you will be able to resist that trend. Perhaps this chapter can help you anticipate and withstand some of the major disappointments you will encounter as you move toward excellence in teaching.

THE TEACHER-HERO

Study the teacher-heroes you meet on your journey toward excellence. Here are some of the characteristics you will notice:

Excellent teachers study their own students. The first thing you may notice when observing a teacher-hero with children is her absolute refusal to give up on a student, ever. Patient and resourceful, she resonates with the idea that you cannot be a teacher unless you are a student of your students. She finds what appeals to that most reluctant student and uses it to bring that child ever closer to loving knowledge.

Excellent teachers want to do more. Her advocacy for her students prompts her to use her own money or the good nature of those she knows to acquire the resources her students need. She constantly works at her craft, wondering what more she can do when she does so much already. The students sense this. The parents bless her for it. Still she frets about what more she can do.

Excellent teachers make careful choices. She may be beloved as a teacher, but she does not require love in order to help her students achieve. The most ornery and unlovable student is as vital to her as the most fawning one. She strives to show every student how learning is connected to life. She is relentless in finding reason to praise. She knows her daily choices and decisions carry a consequence of either life with purpose or dreary emptiness for her students. She chooses wisely.

Excellent teachers respect their profession and their colleagues. She takes risks, even though missed opportunities and errors trouble her conscience. Her passion for achievement may at times isolate her from her colleagues, but she will reach out for support and to offer comfort to those in her profession who care as deeply as she does. Together, they can withstand the inanity and the misery and the anguish and the bureaucracy in teaching to achieve a triumph for the children.

Most telling of all attributes, the teacher-hero shuns the title and shies away from accolades. Drawing attention to her own unique talents as teacher shifts the focus away from students, and to the excellent teacher the children and only the children matter.

PROBLEM: LIMITED PROFESSIONAL PROGRESSION

Teacher-heroes are legendary and numerous. Ask the children, and without guile or agenda they will point them out to you. Ask the administrator or the colleague unsullied by jealousy, and they will name them. And in the "should-be" world, such teacher-heroes would enjoy the same rewards given to those who are deeply talented in the business world: salary bonuses, opportunities to share their leadership theories with younger colleagues, important stakes in the decision-making process of the building.

But in the "can't-be" world the teacher-hero inhabits, there are no preferred parking spots. The teacher-hero will earn what everyone else earns who has her years in the profession and her kind of degree. She will teach the same hours and the same number of courses as a first-year teacher, and she will endure the same inane study hall assignments. If her ambition warrants it, she will progress in the only way we have devised for career progress in American education: to administration, away from children and away from the very substance that brought her to teaching excellence in the first place.

We must devise new and different ways to reward our teacher-heroes. The teacher-hero is not an inexhaustible resource. In a society that recognizes merit with money, and a system chary of offering extra compensation to the excellent teacher, how can such talent be found, nurtured, and retained?

National Board Certification. One possibility for a better form of teacher compensation comes from the National Board for Professional Teaching Standards, which has developed and identified five core attributes of accomplished teaching and the means by which those attributes can be evidenced. The process is rigorous, proven, and national in scope, and some courageous states award a salary adjustment to teachers who achieve national board certification.

Pay Equity. But we should go further than providing salary enhancement to the teacher-hero for achieving National Board certification. The whole traditional structure of teacher compensation based on years of experience and acquisition of collegiate units has become a disservice to teachers. We are all on a continuum of acquired skills. The emerging teacher has different challenges and successes than the veteran teacher does, and it is ludicrous to expect a twenty-two-year-old novice teacher to command the same knowledge base as a twenty-two-year veteran teacher. The teacher's knowledge base grows with time and practice, and teachers should be recompensed when they demonstrate observable improvements in teaching skills, classroom practice, and achieving educational goals.

The private sector has developed new compensation structures based on skills and expertise, goal accomplishment by individuals and by groups. Those deeply concerned about teaching—practitioners and theoreticians, union leaders, rank and file teachers, business leaders, parents—must come together to agree to a necessary task: revamping the teacher compensation system. How many brilliant people do you think we can continue to attract to the teaching profession when there are schools with dilapidated facilities, insufficient resources, limited self-determination, and abysmal compensation? Equity in educational funding is an issue that needs discussion as well, but our immediate need is to attract the truly talented and pay them as well as other professions of great talent for doing the most vital work ever devised—teaching children.

PROBLEM: THE CYNICAL COLLEAGUE

"They pay me whether they learn or not" and "Why are you doing so much? You're making us look bad by comparison." In my years of working with prospective teachers, hearing those words is the single greatest disappointment they express after entering the profession. Colleagues who do not care, are not motivated, go through the motions, offer disservice to children with their cynicism and their distrust—such colleagues will criticize the novice teacher for having energy and positivism. They will warn the new teacher of disappointments to come. Their infectious brand of "who-do-you-think-you-are" is an age-old shield to divert light from their ineptitude. Such teachers will absolutely sap your strength if you allow them to do so.

The majority of the people you meet on your teaching journey will be good, honest, decent, and effective. Many will offer you their ideas and their resources. Some will become your friends for life. But be wary of those in our profession who taint its name. They demoralize both practitioner and child. And, maddeningly, the profession does not have swift mechanisms to deal with them.

Example: On the first day of my tenth year of teaching, our superintendent, an always charming man who dressed in suits the color of autumnal wheat, gathered all the teachers in my district to explain the newest evaluation system the district would employ: "It is just a matter of logic that one of you in here is the worst teacher in the district." Was this comment intended to inform? . . . assist? . . . stigmatize? That was never quite explained to us. Huffy and indignant, we moved off to open our classroom windows and work out that rancid smell each summer layered on the walls, fully believing we were not the worst teachers in the district.

What is more infuriating is that, short of recognizing criminality, any evaluation system, new or not, cannot compel the negative teacher to improve nor threaten that teacher with removal from the profession. There in your midst such teachers will remain, neither inspiring nor struggling to improve nor reflecting on their practice, not really doing anything save serving as an indictment to your diligence. And these representatives of sloth and ignorance who work alongside the industry and excellence of teacher-heroes are paid the same and have exactly the same responsibilities.

Why You Must Remain a Teacher. While you are working and worrying and improving and reflecting, you may get the distinct and unnerving sense that those in your profession who are cynical may be harming scores or hundreds of children yearly. While you become ever more mindful of the damage that can be done by the teaching profession at its worst, you will also be asking yourself who will protect the children? That is why you must remain and persevere.

When You Must Stop Being a Teacher. You may not choose to voice your distaste for your cynical colleagues, and you can leave the room when you hear them blaming parents, society, or anything but themselves for their own failures, but you must hang on until or unless you yourself feel a pull away from the energies that brought you to teaching. If you start to see hopelessness instead of potential in your students' faces, if you start to feel drawn to the anger and negativity of your colleagues, you may have become infected with a cynicism you absolutely cannot hide from your students. They will see it, they will use it to measure their own tentative sense of worth, and they will confirm your prediction that they cannot succeed. If you sense that change, find something else to do with your life. The world is wide and the economy varied, offering you many avenues that can reward and suffice.

How You Can Keep Hope Alive. But if you resent such negativity, if you carry in you some sense of energy and belief in the power of the motivated mind to learn, if you believe that short of pathology your students can learn, then for their sake you must remain. Your stature as a teacher will grow and your development as a hero will continue. You may even wish to broaden your effect within the school community. I hope there is soon a day when your effort and your success will result in an evolution of your role as teacher. Hope drives the excellent teacher onward. Keep it alive in yourself and in the children you encounter. Be part of those who will make the will-be world for this profession.

REFLECTIVE EXERCISES

Study the ineffective teacher. When you come across a teacher whom the children have rejected or about whom colleagues have commented, examine his methods. Listen to him talk about children during lunch. Is there more cynicism than optimism in his words? Learn what not to do and what not to believe from this teacher's example.

Imagine being able to work with children, lead the school, and make decisions that positively impact the educational experience. Could you help younger teachers acquire your sense of mission? Can you imagine an educational community with the flexibility to allow you to develop into a leader on a par with those in the business community? Keep hope alive!

CHAPTER NINE

Reflective Writing Exercises for New and Veteran Teachers

When preparing new teachers, I always insist that the keys to their success will be found in knowing themselves, in knowing which tenets they wish to project to their students and in knowing why they believe those tenets are so important. Students see their teachers as survivors of challenges both academic and personal. They look to their teachers for direction, and they gauge whether the promise of that teacher is dimensional or limited. Students dismiss teachers with specious beliefs about power. And they dismiss teachers who demand respect rather than command it.

Teachers who have a grasp of their own lives, who have reflected on what has occurred and how it has shaped their persona, are able to succeed. They are more comfortable in their own skin, know who they are, and reflect to students a confidence and assurance that offers students direction. The path toward the challenges of adulthood seems safer and more plausible to students when they see someone successful standing at the head of their classrooms.

Acknowledgments: The author thanks Shannon Porter-Busse, Nina Smithe (pseudonym at former student's request), Laura Cottrell, Karen Scheider, and Lauren Levy for permission to reprint their reflections.

Students will naturally gravitate toward adults who offer them a hope that life, with all its burdens, offers reward as well.

"The unexamined life is the life unlived." In reflection and in examination of the teaching life, each one of us can find the reason why we wish to teach.

Here is a selection of preparatory exercises that will allow you to determine who you are, why you are who you are, what it is you may project to students, and what value you may bring to your work with students.

THE ADHESIVE MOMENT

Memory is such a powerful experience. The conduits of memory span stimuli: a smell, a sight, a song, a place, an anniversary, a fabric. Adhesive memories are forged not only by trauma and events of significant impact, but also by the quieter moments whose significance grows as years intervene. This exercise asks you to search your memory with attention to detail.

Think back across your life. You've forgotten many things about your school years, I warrant, but recall a moment when a teacher hurt you by word or deed. I will predict that you can recall just about everything, chapter and verse. Here's mine:

I grew up in the Little Italy West Side of Chicago in a two-flat with a cartage company in the basement run by my uncles. I recall with clarity telling my fourth-grade teacher Sister Mary Astonishment (name changed, of course) that I wanted to teach someday. It was a cloudy day. I wore a white shirt with a blue clip-on tie. She told me, "With your family history, dear, your best hope will be to work with your uncles on their trucks."

Now I know there is absolutely no dishonor in the trucking profession. My point is that my teacher told me that I could not become what I wanted to become, and that memory remains to this day. As teachers, how many children do we damage by adding to their memories something that limits their potential, dams their spirit, clouds their skies?

So the assignment is: recount a memory (that you are comfortable recounting) that holds a certain adhesion to your mind. Why do you think it remains? The adhesive moment exercise brings that moment a relevance that reveals, especially through the passage of time, an understanding of self. In studying and in trying to understand, as one of my own teaching tenets suggests, we can learn how to proceed.

See how much this is evidenced by Shannon's effort, which has the impact of someone who has entered the memory and returned on its other side with an understanding not owned at the onset of the inquiry.

Woman Child
by Shannon Porter-Busse

The abundance of gaily colored bouquets that reside in every doorway matches my mood. The spirit of Mayfest permeates the very Annapolis air, bombarding the tightly closed windows of our snail-like procession of vehicles. We wind slowly through the narrow streets of this tourist town on the way to bury my grandmother. Catherine is entitled to a plot next to her husband in Arlington National Cemetery because of his World War I service before his death thirty-five years ago.

Watching the scenery slide easily out of my view, I try to understand why my aunts and uncles are so entirely dejected. There is the obvious reason of their religion: their strict Catholicism prevents them from believing as Mormons do. But there is something more I cannot comprehend. I did not know my grandmother before she was afflicted by Alzheimer's and therefore cannot recall conflicting images of her.

I vividly recall the story of the day Catherine was diagnosed. A week before, on Mother's Day, she had appeared at her son's door, shaken and sobbing, unable to find her way to church. She had reluctantly consented to accompany him to the doctor's office—with the attitude of an unwilling child being dragged somewhere because her mother felt it was for her good. She politely answered all questions, clearly disgusted with the exercise and convinced the prior week was a natural result of aging. "I am old, and there are certain . . . things that happen. Loss of memory is natural among older people. These doctors don't really care about people. All they want is money."

All logical arguments fell on deaf ears. My grandmother within three years lost all ability to recognize her children or understand their words. In its early stages, the disease merely interfered with the ability to recall dates or the name of once familiar objects. When my mother and I visited her, she was still able to perform most of the tasks necessary for independent living. I allowed this nostalgia to carry me back to my arrival at Catherine's home.

The terrors that had formed in my mind by my mother's warnings were lessened at first sight of the fuchsia ornaments decorating misshapen rhododendrons. The front yard held an extremely large willow whose branches reached toward the ground, forming a dark teepee around its trunk. Crawling inside this sanctuary, I was quite hidden and was able to see a circle of blue. I spied through the branches to where my mother was talking gently with this thin old woman. I imagined I could discern her thoughts, that I could sense her deteriorating mind. I stepped into the sunlight to meet what remained of the woman I called Grandma.

My mother warned me that Grandmother was ill and that she had trouble remembering things. My eleven-year-old mind made no sense of the word Alzheimer's and only knew old people forgot things. I was not prepared, however, when she asked me five consecutive times if we enjoyed our flight and food. I could see her confusion upon hearing the name "Mary Porter." Last names seemed to frighten her, suggesting dangerous strangers who hurt her family.

As we sat in the living room chatting about our trip, Grandma got out of her chair and crossed to the window. Her wraith-like hands went to her hair in agitation. Glaring at the bird feeder in her yard, Catherine turned to the kitchen and returned grasping a broom tightly. "That big bird scares away the little ones. He eats all the food," Catherine stormed out the door. I watched her with wide eyes as she approached the bird feeder and attempted to hit the squirrel on the post that had been stealing food.

My mother put her shaking arm around me and gently reminded me that Grandma was sick and that I should not worry if she called things by the wrong names. When she returned, a heavy silence reflected all the loss that descended between them. My mother could not understand this child before her because she was not willing to release her treasured image of the compassionate, determined mother she once knew. My grandmother was not able to know this strange woman as the spirited blonde she had raised. Unable to watch them struggle with their new roles, I fled.

I wandered freely and with relief among the lilac bushes of the back yard, taking notice of the thin trail between them, perfect for future games of hiding. Noticing the pier nearby, I dashed across buttercups onto the groaning planks to the sailboat bobbing in the choppy waves. I discovered her name was *Silky*. I could imagine her gliding through the waves. Catherine had loved to stand at the helm, grasping the wheel believing she was guiding the vessel. The salt spray would pour across her distant expression, as her son would cautiously correct her efforts at steering.

Returning to the house, the somber mood had brightened and the scene was in harmony with storybook visits to Grandmother's house. The smell of tuna casserole was in the air. Catherine was sitting in an oversized chair, feeling the glossy pages of her picture book, mumbling words of endearment to her bookshelf.

"I love you," my mother's voice unexpectedly called to her from the kitchen.

"I love you, too," Catherine's voice echoed, but I wondered exactly how much of that emotion she was still able to comprehend.

I walked tentatively over to her and sat at her feet. I had an intense desire to create a sanctuary for her where she could recover her true character. I yearned to take her by the hand

and lead her into that haven. I wanted to reach my small arms around her neck and know her as the brilliant teacher, the loving mother. I wanted to see the real grandmother crystallize, but all I could do was sit at her feet and listen to her confusion.

The disease progressed, and within five years my grandmother was no longer able to care for herself. She was given drugs, nameless and horrible, which took her further from us. She became hostile. My mother and her siblings decided to place her in a nursing home.

Monticello was a spacious, strictly run home for the elderly. When my grandmother first arrived there, my brothers and I excitedly welcomed her, expecting to be spoiled by a doting woman. We were quickly disappointed. She could no more bake cookies and buy us treats than she could recognize her own face in the delicate vanity mirror I gave her.

I have no cherished memories of my grandmother. I can only borrow my mother's to gain a sense of who Catherine was and then come to love her true character rather than the empty shell I remember. I remember that betrayal as I am transformed into that confused and bitter fourteen-year-old going to visit my grandmother in the nursing home.

I run my fingers through her snow-white hair, as if this simple motion could help me see beneath the surface and understand. The nursing home staff had given her a terrible perm that left her thinning hair brittle and unmanageable. Catherine's appreciation for finely groomed hair was violated at Monticello. If only I could take her home with me and care for her as she did my mother. I imagine my mother as a schoolgirl, the morning routine leaving her waist-length blonde hair in two French braids. I hear her mother's gentle voice and see her hands as she snips off the blackened ends. I then look around this many-windowed room where grandmother sits in her wheelchair surrounded by other frail residents.

That is the scene that greeted me on my visit. It filled me with ache and pulled tears from me. The slowly deteriorating mind of this once-beloved teacher, whom countless students hailed as brilliant, inspired a deep sense of irony in me that such a gift could be so completely extinguished. As I watched Catherine's trembling hands slowly fold and refold the handkerchief on her lap, the woman who once was appears before me, folding the freshly washed linen in the sunlight. The little girl with the long French braids has matured and stands alongside her, helping take laundry off the line. Their slender forms silhouette the white sheets. As the mother and daughter walk side by side, they discuss literature.

Arlington Cemetery is beautiful. Cherry blossoms drip from the trees. My relatives and I are unable to avert our eyes. We guiltily acknowledge nature's offering. We trail behind the procession, approaching the hole hesitantly. I become dismayed at the many eyes focused upon our small group as just another part of the tourist attraction. I resent that the priest did not know my grandmother. He spits out the same lines he will use at the next hour's funeral. He begins to sprinkle holy water from a cheap plastic bottle, creating small dark spots on the cherry wood coffin I helped my mother select.

I turn to notice my uncle clenching his jaw as he tries to control his emotions. I want to be a small child again and throw my arms around him, explaining in simple terms how Grandma is finally happy. He stands up abruptly and walks up the hill to the cars.

Back in Chicago, as my mother and I return to Monticello to gather Catherine's few belongings, I look around and see that the other nursing home residents seem no less confused or frail. Their eyes, which to me for so long seemed clouded and dim, now hold certain wisdom. I am beginning to see the crisp, white linen among the gray, jumbled fragments of my grandmother's memories. Her experiences as a trusted teacher, a struggling single mother, and a sincere friend lend her an aura that, even in death, commands respect. Clutching this newly discovered reverence, the child I once was runs crying from the room while the woman I am becoming sings softly to a fading image of an old woman in a wheelchair.

I hope you have moments in your careers when you witness such a passing of one of your students from one stage of knowing to another. You will feel humility that your classroom held the promise that such a reflection can be engaged in with confidence. You will feel an honor bestowed upon you.

How will you respond to receiving such an effort? Surely you won't begin with the grammar or narrative structure, although that will have a place at some point. Rather, I hope you will hail the passage that has occurred through reflection. Will you thank the writer for trusting you with a part of what has made her who she is? Will you wonder at this profession where you have had the opportunity to be a healer, to witness the conduit between what they bring into your classroom and what they leave with?

Remember: you can heal and you can harm. Or you can do so little as to be undetected as they pass through your class on their pathway to somewhere else.

TRACKING MY BIAS

Remember that your effectiveness as a teacher will not be gauged by how you work with the students who love you or who make your days run smooth. Those who trouble you, who make your days dark and confused, who confound you, those are the students who will define your effectiveness as a teacher. Moreover, the students most unlike you and most unlike your image of what students should be like, those will be the students who will gauge your talent. Those students will rub against your biases. Let's all take a moment to protest that we love all children and we harbor no biases. Let's exclaim until weary, and then we can think again.

S. I. Hayakawa presented a brilliantly simple theory of how bias is acquired in his work *Language in Thought and Action* ([1949] 1991). Hayakawa termed it the action of "the little man who isn't there." By those we love and admire, or by circumstances in our lives, we acquire in our heads a map of the people who represent the groups for whom we harbor bias.

So many of us recognize the false map that shows the Italians who treat women as objects, the Irish who are drunken romantics or power-mad politicos, the Asians who are overzealous curve-busters. In the context of the high school, the false maps are further delineated. Therein the thespian is the over-dramatic homosexual, the athlete dull and vulgar, the pom-pom student callous and materialistic, the math lover a geek with pocket protectors, the auto shop student a "gear-head" unable to discourse on anything relevant. And, of course, the faculty is clueless and sad without a scintilla of heart or humanity.

On and on the maps are drawn. So when one "sees" someone representing a group one holds in bias, according to Hayakawa, that person is not truly seen. What is seen instead is "the little man who isn't there," which strips the person in front of us of identity and individuality. So our false maps prevent us from seeing the brilliant athletes, the coarse academics, the cheerleaders of great merit and worth, the auto mechanics with a poet's understanding and appreciation of the components of things. But unless and until we rewrite our false maps, we will be denied knowledge of such real persons and banished from real understanding, left to wallow forever in the idiocy of our superficial perceptions of "those people" who behave "that way."

How much waste holding such maps! We who teach must recognize our own false maps, take stock of how we acquired our biases, and study what we are doing to efface those biases. For the teacher with biases who stands in front of students will make those biases as visible as the harvest moon in October.

Prospective teachers find this a difficult reflective exercise because it takes one outside the realm of nostalgia and symbol into the real and the difficult. I used to call this exercise "Why I Hate: What I Must Do," but I changed the title to "Tracking My Bias" after students and prospective teachers claimed they did not really hate anyone or anything. Perhaps hate does escape some, but bias tinges us all. Students and prospective teachers who have undertaken this reflective exercise have written about every ethnic group and some stereotypes as well. One wrote about his distaste for blonde women; many women write about their disgust with men. All say their efforts with their biases are a work in progress, and that is the best that we who prepare future teachers can hope to achieve.

My own tale of how I acquired bias and worked to exorcise it is related to a series of singularly powerful moments woven together.

"Hey, dago, your mother upstairs?" Four black men surround me, their leather jackets smelling of sweat and liquor. "She alone?"

I was eleven and knew how to lie. "She's upstairs with my dad. They're cleaning their guns." A plainclothes cop drives up, honks. They giggle and walk away.

I was not born hating. It was acquired in my years growing up on Chicago's West Side. The Little Italy of my youth was in disarray as I entered my teens. Graffiti and urine collected in the doorway of our two-flat on DeKalb Street. "Damn *melanzana*," my father would say (eggplant in Italian bastardized in pronunciation to "mullajan" or "mulley," the shorthand map my father and uncles gave to me about the blacks encroaching into our neighborhood).

Events occurred—my jacket ripped, my sister harassed. I remembered the Sisters taking us seventh graders to the tony suburb of Oak Brook to see a movie and afterwards to drive around the neighborhood. "Study hard and some day you'll live in a place like this," they promised us.

Who were they kidding? When Dr. King was murdered, Western Avenue went ablaze. My father, uncle, brother and I guarded our home through the night. Gone were the summer evenings when overcome by heat we would sleep out on the back porch. Gone were the summer evenings when Dad would take us to the grassy lawn around Adler Planetarium to roll around and laugh and fish for smelt or throw stones in the lake. When a National Guardsman with full battle fatigues, helmet, and bayonet-prepared rifle ordered me to go home when I went to get milk from Bill's Grocery, I knew those days were gone. First we fought to stay, and then we fled—Italians scattering to the suburbs: Cicero, Berwyn, Melrose Park, Elmwood Park.

In Elmwood Park I was the darkest person those kids had ever seen. "Bantu" became my nickname after a character from the novel *Durango Street,* assigned by a well-intentioned nun to give us a flavor of the suffering in the ghetto.

I thought I knew from suffering then, whisked away from the neighborhood I loved because of the *melanzana.* My dad drove us around River Forest on summer evenings, showing us the homes of Mafiosi. "Here's where Paul 'the Waiter' Ricca lives. There's Sammy 'Momo' Giancana's place. Tony Accardo lives here." We had a stock dialogue as he drove away: "But are they all really happy?" my father would ask. I'd say to myself, "Hell, yes, look where they live!" My mother's family cemetery plot in Mt. Carmel stood around a tight corner from Alfonso Capone's himself. Few know where Scar Face is buried, his grave guarded by high bushes. As a boy I would hide behind them and hug Alfonso's stone. "*Faccia Sfregio,*" I whispered, "the *melanzana* took me away from my home. Whadd'ya gonna do?" If he knew, he wasn't saying.

So the years passed in my all-white suburb, black population in 1968: zero. We kids would burn together in our shared hatred of what "they" did and could do. All of us seemed touched by threat, by violence, by sadness, by ignorance and obstinacy, full of posture.

College began the effacement of my hatred. After Bobby Kennedy's death in 1968 the word was out—someone was trying to get us. The Summer of Love came and went without me. Kent State enraged. Jackson State made it serious. I received my draft lottery number in 1972: 314. No 'Nam for this *faccia bruta*! Music changed me, Vietnam changed me, protesting changed me.

Lawrence McCutcheon changed me.

Lawrence worked with me when I spent a desultory summer on a loading dock for the University of Illinois at Chicago, delivering office supplies to the various departments.

Lawrence was black and angular, and I avoided him with evil stares. He played up to my bias, humming as we passed, changing the radio dial to Marvin Gaye on WVON after I tuned Led Zeppelin on WXRT. Smiling, he'd ask if I wanted to go out to lunch. "NO," I was quick to reply. But work does something to you. You can't help but be together, swinging boxes of paper onto wooden dollies to wheel onto delivery trucks, riding elevators. Lawrence wouldn't let up. "A beer after work?" I finally said yes on a rainy June Tuesday.

"So what has you all eaten up inside?" he asked me.

I laid out my map as completely as I could. All the offenses, to me and to my family, were retold.

A very few times in your life, you will be changed by a single sentence. Lawrence McCutcheon gave me a chance to survive when, after my bitter, tear-inducing tale, he replied:

"Hell, man, it weren't black people who did this to you. It was evil people who happened to be black."

Like a shot, like a clear shot, those words entered me, and began relaxing the exhaustion hate creates.

*   *   *

Years later: the family at Sunday dinner. The pasta smoke rises to the ceiling as it has done for centuries in Italian households. Laughter and wine.

My sister, now married with three kids, announces to us that she and her husband are adopting their fourth. Cheers abound. Yes, she was planning to adopt an African-American child. Silence.

Silence.

My father nodded, said little. While washing dishes I ask her the only sentence on the subject I ever uttered:

"You sure about this?"

"I have my reasons," she responded.

In our large family, many members made their biases known. My father remained silent until my sister's father-in-law said how stupid an idea this was, and only someone like my sister could think of such a thing. Well, then my father thought this was the best idea he ever heard of, because his daughter thought it.

Much can be argued well on both sides on the subject of interracial adoption. Both sides valid, but that is not part of this story. But in the years before he died, I just wish you could have seen my father playing with his absolute favorite grandson, stuck like Velcro to my father's leg, their laughter booming around the house on Sunday afternoons. On one of those afternoons, I caught my sister throwing me a look, as if to ask, "See? See?"

*   *   *

Years later: my father lay in a Loyola Hospital bed, waiting for coronary bypass. I don't know how it goes in your family, but in mine every family member within hailing distance feels honor bound to go to the hospital when one of us ails. So in the outer room at 6:30 that morning stood dozens of aunts, uncles, and *cousines,* arguing about where to buy the best *mortadella* for the afternoon lunch.

Inside the room was private and quiet: my mother, my father, my sister and brother and me, tight as tourniquets, silent. Then in walked Mr. Jerry, six feet, three inches, so black he looked blue, entering to prepare my father for surgery. He opened my father's hospital gown to shave his chest. And sighed.

"Why don't I ever get a Chinaman to prepare with one chest hair? I always have to get you Eye-talians with more hair on your chest than on your head."

Our eyes moved toward him slowly. My sister giggled.

"Yessir," Mr. Jerry continued, shaving and humming, "I'm good with a razor. They put me on work release from the prison in Joliet so I could come here and impress you all with my technique."

Now we were all smiling. My mother, ever ready to contribute to racial harmony, responded, "You know, my daughter adopted a black child."

Mr. Jerry smiled and whistled. "Now, how you know that baby's adopted? Maybe she had a hankering for brown sugar?"

Now even my father was laughing. My mother searched her purse for the family photo.

"Here we all are," she said.

"Nice," said Mr. Jerry.

"And this one is . . ."

"I know which one, ma'am." Mr. Jerry replied, laughing. "OK, everyone, time now for kissy-kissy. Me and papa here got to go."

We lined up to say see you soon. I'll never forget my father and mother kissing last, with that look between them you'd hope to have with someone in your life, when it all counts and life and love and promise together can be held in that look.

I'll also never forget my father being wheeled away by Mr. Jerry, both of them guffawing, heading for quadruple bypass and five more years of life.

Days later in recovery, Mr. Jerry stopped by to see how my father was doing.

"When I'm out of here, Jerry, you come over to the house for pasta," my father said.

Mr. Jerry gave a slow and sad smile. "Are people like me allowed where people like you live?"

And my father, five years before his death, having fought in the Second World War, having his photography business crumble, working two jobs to support us, having witnessed both spoken and unspoken agonies over the years, having had a hand in teaching me how to hate, who packed us to the suburbs to escape, who laughed and laughed with his black grandson, said to Mr. Jerry, "In my house you are always welcomed."

One person at a time is how the bridges that separate us are built. One person at a time is how they are dismantled.

The reason bias proliferates is that we are not prone to place ourselves in positions of actually looking at each other as people. It is far simpler to categorize and assume than it is to individualize and discover.

Watch how tempted you will be to fall on your preconceptions and false map biases in the classrooms. The teaching task is so exhausting, the demands so relentless that temptation will rise merely from your weariness. The moment you allow your biases to surface, your students will notice it. Students are more attuned to that part of your mien than any other aspect of your teaching. They take for granted your subject matter mastery. They will give you license to falter in your class structure on occasion. They will be quiet when they sense you need them to be (unless you have lost their regard, for then they will revel in your confusion). But demonstrate bias and nothing can camouflage your bias.

It is vital that you examine "the little men who [aren't] there" in your mind. We all must recognize our false maps, take stock of how we acquired our biases, and study what we are doing to efface those biases.

THE AUTOBIOGRAPHICAL FAIRY TALE

As a young teacher, I experimented with ways to get students to open up, to abandon the artificial selves so many don in an attempt to move away from serious reflection. The comfortable, structure-laden "In my paper I will compare basketball to football" formulaic paragraphs that pretend to be essays are the comfortable refuge of many students. I hoped to convince them that their writing assignments were photographs of the interior of their mind and heart. While most photographs of ourselves make us cringe, with practice we acquire an understanding of our true selves. I sought to move beyond the stock and the blurry in essay assignments.

One early successful project focused on the fairy tale. We read tales from the Brothers Grimm and Mother Goose in an effort to see how moral was embedded in the tale. Then I asked them to write a fairy tale that would impart a lesson they would wish their children to learn. So they would start in reverse order, crafting a moral that meant something to them, then animate the moral with a fable they'd create. What would surface were essays on the nature of Tommy the Goldfish, who was your average ordinary goldfish living well in his goldfish world with his friends happily until one day when Tod showed up. Tod was a goldfish that looked different—a ripped fin, a different hue. The other goldfish were suspicious of Tod and didn't want him playing their goldfish games. Then came the day when Tommy got to see Tod's true nature. He was just like the other goldfish. Tommy told his friends to back off. Tod was cool, and all remained well in the goldfish world.

Such assignments were done well enough. The students offered a glimpse of their values and activated them by symbolic manipulation of the structures inherent in fairy tales. But the assignment did not approach what I sought.

About this time my own children were young and of the age to hear stories. My forays into the library for bedtime reading material brought me to a realization of how today's society is reflected in children's literature. Looking for variations of "Rapunzel" or "The Fox and the Grapes" brought me to titles such as "Daddy Doesn't Live Here Anymore" and other announcements of the scary new order. On one of these library hunts I happened upon Bruno Bettleheim's work *The Uses of Enchantment* ([1975] 1989). Bettleheim's writing and life work has spiraled into neglect after allegations about him surfaced after his death. His psychological interpretations of traditional fairy tales were also rebuffed in his time. So it was in amusement that I read his theory of Rapunzel, the story of a girl locked in a tower by a fearful parent to prevent her from meeting suitors. The plan was repelled by Rapunzel, who grew her hair long enough to allow her suitor to climb up the tower to her aid. Bettleheim felt this was the tale of a young woman whose parents vainly attempted to stop their daughter from reaching sexual maturity. Such an attempt is futile, Bettleheim urged, because children know instinctively such attempts are wrong and should be repelled, for no person can prevent another from achieving his or her destiny as a sexually active person.

Bettleheim theorized that traditional fairy tales embedded problems within them, involving children otherwise left to their own devices to solve. With the help of the wise owl or the babbling brook, such answers were provided. Children who like a particular tale, Bettleheim wrote, did so because the imbedded problem in the tale matched the problem they unconsciously recognized existing in their own lives and through the retelling of such a tale sought resolution.

Now I had trouble thinking that my daughter, when she asked me to reread "Rapunzel," was plotting her rebellion. But reading his work brought me to rethink the fairy tale as a conduit for reflection. The genre uses symbol manipulation that can allow one's values to surface. Using symbol manipulation in writing reflectively would allow students to write their feelings camouflaged in a symbol system they could easily interpret. From these thoughts was borne perhaps the most successful writing assignment I ever used with students: write the story of your life as if it were a fairy tale. Giving students the authority to select the moments of their life they wish to convey and the freedom to create a symbol system that would animate the people and events in their chosen moments gave them a great freedom. They could write with passion and clarity cloaked in the fairy tale world they could understand.

The quality of the writing I receive from such an exercise is almost always stunning. They also were often times difficult to interpret, since the author holds the key to understanding each particle of the fairy tale world created and the meaning imbedded within it. But I found myself not caring if I understood every nuance. What was important was their reflecting, and by such reflecting learning how to proceed.

One student of mine was particularly opaque in her reflective written work. Her interpretive skills with literature were excellent yet early personal reflections offered little. In introspective writing it was essential for me to inform my students that they controlled the boat they rowed. Nothing that made them uncomfortable reflecting needed to be forced out. All moments take time to digest, and the meaning of those moments comes in revelation in slow degrees as the years pass the veils of introspection over them. I forced no skeleton shaking through the assignments I gave. Then I assigned the autobiographical fairy tale.

I have already told you about moments in your career when you will be blown away by the work of your students. Years later, rereading what Nina wrote still sends chills through me. In terms of its understanding of self and of that time in her life, its clarity and insight stuns. Seeing such power in the writing of an eleventh-grade student brought me to always believe in the ability of young people to reflect upon the circumstances of their lives and seek through that understanding a pathway to continuing.

All one needs to know in glimpsing Nina's tale is that the oak tree represents high school and all the caterpillars upon it students.

A Tale
by Nina Smithe

Well then, my child, you tell me you are unhappy, you, who continually grasp for things beyond your reach, not realizing that they are unattainable and, if stripped of their glittery façade, undesirable. You, curiously afraid of others and wishing with all your might to rise above them, as if they were something detestable, alienating yourself behind a wall of perfection. Let me tell you a story, and listen carefully to what I say, child, before it is too late for you as it is now too late for me.

Several years ago in a small garden near the gnarled roots of an oak tree, a colony of caterpillars lived. The tree was only a temporary stopping point though, until they acquired their strong, splendid wings, which would enable them to venture into the sky. The caterpillars often dreamed of their future, but for now they were content with their simple lives and enjoyed crawling in mud and among the blades of grass.

However, one caterpillar (how much reminiscent of you) would struggle to the topmost branches of the oak and gaze longingly at the birds and butterflies, craving to join them as they freely soared through the air yet, at the same time, wanting desperately to belong to the group of caterpillars on the ground. She was somehow a little different and the other caterpillars sensed this and rarely approached her. Perhaps her thoughts and dreams were so much more extreme and painful that she was no longer a part of their world. Her loneliness, though, was partly her fault, for whether due to weakness or fear, she rarely attempted to climb down from the lofty branches and speak with the others.

Perhaps she hadn't meant to form it, but nevertheless, a cocoon gradually built up around her, layer by layer, until it was almost impenetrable. There she nestled, snugly enveloped in an illusion of warmth and love, sheltered from the cold air and quizzical, harsh stares of the others. Inside her cocoon, she planned and dreamed and fastidiously selected her beautiful colors, carefully rearranging them, attempting to find the pattern that best suited her. When she would finally emerge, she would dazzle the world with her radiant magnificence, soaring above the heads of the common caterpillars, who would look up in awe at her beauty and feebly reach out to her.

Sometimes, making a special effort, a few of the caterpillar's old friends would struggle up the tree to her cocoon and try to coax her out. But she would always decline, being completely absorbed in her plans. She would tell herself that she had no need of love, especially from the ignorant little caterpillars on the ground. But she was mistaken, for inside she craved it more than anything else. Perhaps she imagined she could only find happiness by attaining perfection. She was oblivious to the fact that this was the very thing that drove it away. Isolated in her lofty tree, the cocoon imperceptibly began to harden, and with it, so did the caterpillar's emotions and ability to care and love. But still she continued her vain pursuit of unattainable beauty, loathing her own imperfections as well as the blemishes of the other caterpillars, which were easily perceived when they tried to come close to her.

Meanwhile, the rest of the colony squirmed among the roots of the oak tree out in the sun. Unsheltered by cocoons, they were often cut as they crawled about, but these scratches soon healed and were replaced by stronger, wiser fibers through their exploits. They discovered which leaves were delicious and which ones would make them sick. And, most important of all, they learned to laugh at, and eventually love, their own ugliness.

One day a small tree animal, perhaps hungry or simply unaware of all the elaborate dreams encased in the cocoon, gingerly picked it up between its front teeth, chewed it, and sent it sliding down its throat into a vitriolic pool of stomach acids. The other caterpillars were shocked and a little saddened by this occurrence, but in time, these feelings passed and she was forgotten. What is one dead caterpillar out of the millions that inhabit the earth? And she had never been a very friendly caterpillar anyway.

So, my child, you ask what happened to the other caterpillars? Well, a few always remained in their earth-bound forms, but most, without any special planning or sacrifice, eventually blossomed into colorfully winged butterflies, although a little less dazzling than the lonely caterpillar's ideal.

Think carefully about what I have told you. You must help yourself, child, no one else can—least of all me. For I can shed no tears over your misfortunes nor smile at your triumphs. My heart is encased in an iron cocoon that I, in my folly, put there by myself.

Author's Note: The author wishes to thank the essayist for permission to reprint "A Tale." The essay originally appeared in *The Journal of the Illinois Council for the Gifted* (1990).

When you establish an atmosphere of trust and responsible risk taking, using a framework for your lessons that hearkens back to a set of tenets you hold as essential to your reason to teach, then the possibility emerges that you will be seen as an instructor worth focused attention. The results can be effort from your students that far exceeds expectation. You show them the reflection of your tenets, and they reflect back their growing sense of understanding, through your work, of who they are and what they must do to continue growing.

I encourage you to try this reflective exercise yourself. The act of selecting moments and assigning symbols to them, and the manner in which you manipulate them, will speak clearly about your pathway heretofore.

Why do so? How can you begin to approach an understanding of your students without an understanding of yourself? How will you recognize their struggle for becoming if they cannot see you as someone who has undergone that struggle? That you have survived personal and professional challenge will influence them. They will understand the necessary discipline of your study as they see you as worthy of trust and emulation. They will see scientific method as a function of the excellence you exhibit. They will honor language precision as the vehicle for your beliefs. How much have you emulated those you admire? It is the necessary step to acquiring your own persona. What results is a combination of the stages of your life, what you have endeavored to study and taken in as your own style of thought and action. This is the teacher you can be if you see teaching as the result of a conscious act of reflection and consideration about what you value and have learned from life. Teachers of limited ability actively decline to act upon set tenets. They respond to reactionary assumptions about students and act in a manner that will produce the limited results they believe exist in them. They do not trust students to push themselves to greater levels of achievement. Because these teachers will not, their students can not.

How many classrooms have you observed where you have seen deadening instruction occurring, lifeless manipulations of time and activity connected to no set tenet, no framework—the teacher who can not or will not move to a different set of actions or structures beyond rote memory and diluted expectations? The students respond as they perceive, and you wish to scream. Right at this moment, today or tomorrow's day, in countless classrooms across this nation such dread continues.

Is that the legacy you wish to continue? If not, get busy knowing thyself, and learning where you need to go to develop as a teacher of dimension and substance to your students.

TEACHING AS SONG: PUT YOUR REASONS FOR TEACHING INTO A LYRIC

Our teaching lives are a type of song, sung in a place where others witness. If you sing with readiness and with spirit, your classroom can become a place of order, where one may find a deepened sense of what it means to be human.

For many years I have asked students and prospective teachers to write songs and sing them to their peers. That seems to me to be a distillation of the teaching challenge: to allow themselves to be open, to be seen and heard, to send forth from their mouths a voice that through spirit attempts to bring order to their world. I asked them to write songs about why they wanted to teach; what about teaching compelled them to study further.

The act of singing their songs has always been a gracious, cathartic event. In those venues, we did not care about the quality of one's voice, for we are all in the process of perfecting our voices as teachers and as people. I conclude this chapter with lyrics of past prospective teachers. I invite you to consider and craft your own song. This you will be doing during the entire extent of your life as a teacher.

Music Is the Voice of All Sorrow, All Joy
by Lauren Levy

Twenty-five pair of eyes

Waiting for an answer.

Why do they think I'm so wise?

How can they understand

That I am just a dreamer like them?

I am just a believer like them.

I am as weak as them.

A young boy comes before me,

I was still in my youth,

Wanting to know all about life,

Unable to hear the truth.

His gazing stare, his aching heart,

All the defenses I had began to fall apart.

They say to teach is to touch lives.

Who knew it would be like this?

Who knew the love that would abound?

I hardly knew the young boy I would miss.

The shot rang out, I heard his cry

The day I learned my student died.

Every Child
by Karen Scheider

A child who's never heard "You did a good job,

I'm proud of you." He's always trying.

Never feeling as if he matters.

His parents fail to make him know he's loved.

Never felt a sense of hope.

Grant this child's wish; change his empty, cold world.

Be his hero.

Born into a place that offers no safety,

Will her family eat, her daddy come home?

Will she fade away?

All she wants is love and certainty,

A place to shed frightened tears.

Be this child's friend, offer her loving care.

Be her shelter.

All we are assured is that some people get lost along the way.

But don't decide this fate yourself by choosing to turn and look away.

We are called to love,

Let's start by offering all we can

To the innocent children waiting to be formed.

Be their teacher.

Hope is only lost if we allow it

To exit from their souls.

Every spoken word can make the difference

To the roads they choose.

Give of yourself to children yearning to be saved from emptiness.

Offer all you can.

You can save a child's dreams, her hope, her faith:

A child's life.

The Lesson
by Laura Cottrell

Are you ready to teach?

Why are you playing around?

It's a serious profession,

Don't need promises that fall to the ground.

Are you ready to teach

With its responsibilities?

Don't know the meaning of scholar,

Can't get by with inactivity.

You say you don't need direction,

That you've figured it out,

But if you listen to wisdom,

You'll succeed, no doubt.

Are you ready to teach

With all your negativity?

I hope you change your position

To ignite your inner beauty.

They say that life is a circle

And what you sow you shall reap,

Well if you try to play your teachers now

What makes you think your turn will be sweet?

I'm not trying to preach

But are you really ready to teach?

I hope so much for you to succeed. Indeed, teaching is the challenge you have set for yourself. You will learn that the children indeed do call. Yet the call is muted, disguised in pose and bravura, camouflaged by unconcern and apathy. So much damage may have already been done to their creativity and their capacity to believe in themselves by the teachers in their past that by the time you meet them, they may already have written you off. Disappointment may have led them to anticipate that you too will falter, give up on them, sell them short, or walk away. Disappointment may increase their cynical belief that school is useless outside the curricula of the hallways. But their very reticence is a call for you to act. Their insolence is a call for you to proceed with intelligence and meaning. Their silence is a call for you to demonstrate that their lives do have meaning.

Start by walking into your own classroom resolved that you will not give up on a single child. You may enter your classroom thinking "If only they will move halfway, I will meet them." They are looking at you thinking "If only this one can show some care, and move halfway toward me, I will approach." You have only to move with a plan and an attuned ear, staunch belief, and resilience. Your efforts will be rewarded many times.

I started this book by asking you if you think you will be ready. No one ever really is totally ready for the immensity and the complexity of teaching. But you can increase the odds for success. Have a plan. Have a reason to stand up in front of your students. Let your every action be based on a tenet. Listen to them. Learn from them. You can and will find moments in your classroom when you are absolutely sure you are saving lives and healing wounds. You can almost hear it when it happens.

When you do hear, when you do see, you will be ready.

CHAPTER TEN

Creating Programs for Teacher Preparation

The Programs of the Golden Apple Foundation in Illinois

> *I promise to try as well as I can to succeed in college, to learn my subject well, and to learn how to teach and inspire children. I promise to work to become a role model others would be proud to emulate. I promise these goals in the name of my family, by whose example I arrived at this time and place in my life. I promise these goals in the name of the children I've yet to meet and those who died or were lost before I was ready to help them.*
>
> —Golden Apple Scholars of Illinois pledge

My aspiration to help prepare teachers was launched in 1987 by my inclusion in the second class of teachers chosen for the Golden Apple Award by the then Foundation for Excellence in Teaching.

Each year the Golden Apple Foundation for Excellence in Teaching selects from Cook, Lake, and DuPage Counties in Illinois 10 teachers who represent outstanding teaching ability. The original intent of the organization was purely to reward teachers, but those teachers pushed to become more than what I once indelicately called "hood ornaments for education."

The 20 Fellows in the early years of the Academy of Educators spoke as one about our arduous path to teaching, the isolation of our early years, and the frustrations that led us to consider leaving the profession. We also spoke of our instinctive ability to note which of our students would make terrific teachers, and the limitation of our influence to inspire those students to take that path.

RECRUITING PRE-INDUCTION TEACHERS-TO-BE

The 10 high school teachers selected in 1987 took on creating a teacher recruitment program. We felt that if there was a pathway established to recognize young people with nascent teaching talent, selected as the best by a process modeling the manner we were selected as Fellows, and if those selected were presented with an augmentation to traditional teacher preparation, those students would succeed as the next generation of great teachers.

We devised a plan whereby those Scholars, as we called them, would receive early induction into teaching situations and methods. We felt that by association with award-winning teachers who took an interest in developing their talents, those promising prospective teachers would develop into career teachers. We also suspected that the strong esprit de corps that would develop among cadres of these Scholars would encourage and support them through the challenges of college and the demands of the early years in the profession.

The result was our creation of the Golden Apple Scholars of Illinois. With the help of Mike and Pat Koldyke, the founder and first director of the program, respectively, we were able to acquire funding to select 15 Scholars for the first Summer Institute in 1989 at the campus of the University of Illinois at Chicago. With great excitement we brought these young people together to experience firsthand the heartbreaks and triumphs of urban education by observing and interacting with Chicago Public School children. The late afternoons were spent in methodology courses offered by the Fellows, and a Reflective Seminar series designed to debrief their observation experiences and to foster in them, from an early age, the capacity to reflect on teaching styles and view teaching as a mission. Professor Bill Ayers of the University of Illinois at Chicago was instrumental in helping us define the uniqueness of the Summer Institute concept.

Through private funding we selected another 20 Scholars in 1990, 22 in 1991, and 25 in 1992. The program expanded to include camp counseling. By this time the success of our efforts, and the intervention by Mike Koldyke with the administration of then Governor Jim Edgar, brought us the distinction of expanding to a program that would select Scholars from throughout the state, tripling the size of our program.

We began selecting 60 Scholars a year in 1993, and did so every year until we picked 75 in 1999 and 100 in 2000. From a program that operated on $65,000 of private and corporate contributions we grew to a program that received $3.9 million dollars in 2002 from the Illinois State Board of Education and the Illinois Board of Higher Education, along with continuing contributions from corporations and individuals.

With over 690 Scholars now in the program, with over 225 of them now teaching, with another 100 chosen each year, the Scholars program has grown into a premier pre-induction teacher preparation program. Since 1993 our simple idea has attracted over $17 million to the cause of quality teaching! The power of words!

PREPARING EXCELLENT TEACHERS FOR SCHOOLS OF NEED

The mission of the Golden Apple Scholars of Illinois program is to recruit and prepare high school graduates (and, in a recent addition, college sophomores through a supplemental pathway) who have the promise for successful careers as excellent teachers in service to children in schools of need throughout Illinois.

Recognizing the critical shortage of teachers in Illinois schools, especially minority and male teachers, we began to vigorously recruit talented high school students to become educators in Illinois communities with the greatest need. The Golden Apple Academy provides appropriate methodology and subject matter through its Summer Institutes to inspire Scholars to develop the qualities and knowledge needed to excel.

The institutes give methodology that works and add the real-life experiences of recognized superior teachers to the research learned in college, a combination sorely lacking in the traditional teacher preparation pathway. Without that combination so many aspiring young people are absolutely leveled by the challenges of learning to become a teacher: crushing paperwork, societal indifference if not abject hostility, and a gnawing sense of isolation. No wonder so many young teachers leave the profession in the first five years! The fact that over 95 percent of the Golden Apple Scholars who enter teaching remain in teaching is testament to the value of advanced preparation before and careful mentoring after.

After our initial partnership in 1989 with 4 Illinois universities, in 2002 our partnership extended to 48 of the 55 teacher-preparation institutions in Illinois, with more each year joining our effort to bring a new and augmented form of teacher preparation in Illinois.

Our program is straightforward: we provide much-needed funds and unparalleled pre-induction teaching experience to our Scholars. They agree in return to teach in an Illinois school we designate as a "school of need" for five years within eight years after graduating. We classify schools of need in Illinois by two criteria:

1. Schools designated with Chapter 1 status (known as the Perkins Loan List) by the Department of Education, signifying that a certain percentage of students in such schools come from families whose incomes are defined by the federal government as low; or

2. By scores achieved by pupils on state standardized tests (PSAE/ISAT).

All Scholars contractually agree to teach for five years in Illinois schools so designated in return for the award of $28,000.

Describing the type of person we seek to attract to this program is complicated. You look for people who have the potential to be great teachers. What does that mean? The attributes of a potentially excellent teacher are complex and interwoven. We believe Scholars must be experts in their particular disciplines, possess excellent work habits, and exhibit a capacity for hard work and serious effort. Respect for others, scrupulous attention to assignments, punctuality, a positive self-concept, and a desire to teach, all are necessary traits. In addition, we hope to help Scholars develop the ability to make decisions, handle stress, deal assertively with the demands of a complex profession, and develop the skills necessary to maintain a healthy outlook.

An excellent teacher-to-be must exhibit intellectual curiosity and must be a compassionate, resilient person, aware of the travails of growing up, sensitive to the problems of young people and concerned about their well being. The essence of the excellent teaching spirit—a core of goodness—is the hallmark of a Scholar. We want to prepare Scholars to enter a classroom and exemplify this spirit.

GOLDEN APPLE SUMMER INSTITUTES

The heart of our program, known as Summer Institute (SI), is a series of four consecutive summer experiences that are planned, taught, and administered by the Fellows of the Golden Apple Academy and assisted by teaching Scholars. Every class at SI has as its basic element the demonstration of the art and craft of teaching.

Golden Apple Scholars convene for the first two summers after selection at Chicago's DePaul University for a six-week, paid residential internship. In the first two summers of the program, Scholars are involved in teaching settings with Chicago school children in the morning and take courses reflecting on the morning experiences and on the art of teaching in the afternoon. The third summer's experience offers the Scholars an opportunity to tailor their own learning experience, while the fourth summer experience is a two-week residential institute at a host university that provides final preparation for entering student teaching and the teaching profession.

We have expanded to provide a fifth Summer Institute, known as CORE (Center for Ongoing Renewal and Enrichment), offered for teaching Scholars to provide opportunities to reflect on the early years of teaching and methods to improve and enhance their teaching. These are the tenets of the Summer Institute:

- To provide Scholars with intensive, practical classroom experience combined with training and reflection based on those experiences
- To create a supportive network of peers and mentors
- To inspire Scholars to bring their special talent and training into schools of defined need in communities throughout Illinois

- To develop in Scholars a teaching style which encourages self-respect, respect for children, and awareness of diverse learning styles and cultural backgrounds
- To provide a model of teacher preparation that addresses the needs of a multicultural and international society
- To create a nurturing environment where Scholars can continue to develop as caring and compassionate individuals and teachers

As a result of this program each Scholar can

- Accumulate up to 450 hours or more of classroom and field experiences and teaching practicum during the four Summer Institutes held prior to student teaching,
- Develop an understanding of his or her own and other people's attitudes, cultures, and beliefs,
- Develop a "tool kit" of teaching tips, techniques, experiences, and lesson plan ideas that enables the Scholar to succeed in teaching culturally, ethnically, racially and linguistically diverse students,
- Become part of a collaborative group of peers who understand the challenges and rewards of teaching in high-need schools, and
- Demonstrate a commitment to teaching students in Illinois schools of need.

As a result of teaching for five years, we hope that Scholars will be able to

- Foster collaboration within a school environment and fully engage in the teaching profession,
- Internalize the spirit reflected in the Summer Institute and continue to value the role of "reflective practitioner" as a method to use in analyzing personal growth as a teacher, and
- Become a catalyst for educational change in Illinois.

This program, albeit life-changing and tremendously affirming for those who participated in it, did not develop without its challenges and turmoil. Selecting Scholars from across the state—rich mouse, poor mouse, city mouse, suburb mouse, country mouse, palace high school mouse, dilapidated high school mouse, white, black, brown and yellow mouse—brought unique challenges to our model.

Struggling with the issues of racial discrimination and poverty has helped to define these young people as prospective teachers. Those struggles, and the seemingly endless conversations between Scholars and Fellows, have brought a wisdom and an experiential strength that the Scholars in turn bring to their first teaching assignments, qualities we proudly witness in our visits to Scholars at their first schools.

APPRENTICESHIP AND MASTERY

Our conversations with principals and department chairs return the same request: send us more like these! The University of Illinois at Chicago agreed to study the Scholars program to determine the advantage being a Scholar has brought to the classrooms where these Scholars teach (Center for Urban Research and Development, 2001).

These results, published in April, 2001, brought efficacy to our work. Golden Apple Scholars were found to be superior in dispositions most likely to result in effective teaching. They were three times as likely to use varied techniques. They showed superior teaching performance in comparison to traditionally prepared teachers. The study championed the fourteen years put into refining the program. Harvard University further honored our efforts by naming the Golden Apple Scholars of Illinois one of 15 finalists of 1,300 programs nominated nationwide for consideration for the prestigious Innovations in American Government Award sponsored by the Ford Foundation.

The very heart of this program, what makes it work, was the idea that prospective teachers must apprentice with master teachers who help them understand the need to establish tenets and frame the work they will do with children around strongly held philosophic principles. The many Fellows who have shared their vision with the Scholars have helped them hone their own teaching methods and philosophy.

I am proud that I have taught every Scholar ever named, and in the cases of those who have succeeded in reaching their dream—to teach—I've gained satisfaction from helping them to view the profession as more than job, closer to mission. Scholars see at seventeen that children, especially children living in poverty, can very well be lost if their education does not bring them hope, a means to improve their mind, and a capacity and appetite for learning. The Scholars themselves speak passionately of those in their lives who lost the struggle for purpose and meaning. With their energy, these teachers are beginning to have positive effect on the children of Illinois. I hope their ambitions carry them to positions of educational leadership. Thus is the crooked made straight.

I present the story of this program because I believe its structure can be used as a template elsewhere around the nation. Organizations of teachers should come together with a mission: attract others to the profession, use our strengths as classroom teachers to help these prospective educators acquire an augmented set of preparatory experiences. We will gain not just more teachers, but more teachers committed to, dedicated to, teaching.

RECRUITING ALTERNATIVE CERTIFICATION TEACHERS

In 1996 I left teaching and joined the Golden Apple Foundation full-time to direct the Golden Apple Scholars program and to help create another teacher preparation program for mid-career adults 25–55 who wish to change careers and join the profession, especially in the much needed areas of mathematics and science. With my colleague and dear friend Peg Cain, Foundation president from 1995–2000, we together fashioned an alternative certification pathway for these prospective teachers. We coined the acronym GATE (Golden Apple Teacher Education) for the project and began crafting its structure. We proposed a yearlong process leading to the recommendation of successful GATE interns to the state for certification.

Our first challenge was in finding a university partner. Nine were approached and turned down our idea, claiming it was too radical, too dangerous, too political a concept. This, for two former English teachers not far removed from teaching Dante to high school seniors, was the beginning of our political baptism. We were able to achieve a fruitful partnership with Northwestern University, thanks to the strong participation of its Dean of the School of Education and Social Policy, Penelope Peterson, who bravely stayed with us despite the rancor of her peers to our idea.

The selection process we devised was a three-stage competitive process:

1. A transcript evaluation by Northwestern faculty and Golden Apple. While most candidates accepted at this stage will have met or nearly met general education requirements, a waiver of some general education requirements was sought to gain the flexibility to further scrutinize candidates of exceptional promise, especially those with mathematics and science training.

2. An application evaluation of six full-length essays and three letters of recommendation. Patterned after the application we devised for the Golden Apple Scholars program, we sought to gauge through the essays and letters a measurement of the candidate's literacy and ability to work with urban school children.

3. The Haberman interview. This process, developed by Professor Martin Haberman of the University of Wisconsin at Milwaukee, a famed proponent of alternative teacher certification concepts, is already used with remarkable success nationwide in determining the likelihood of a candidate's success in working with urban school children.

Throughout the process, our primary focus would be to find candidates interested in and suited to teaching mathematics and science, though our intent is to find outstanding candidates for other levels and subjects as well.

The first phase of the program we devised consisted of an eight-week session with teams of two interns placed in Chicago Public School summer school classrooms where master teacher practitioners teach an enrichment program. These master practitioners would be chosen from the ranks of those who have received the Golden Apple Award from the Foundation and other recognized outstanding teachers. The GATE interns will be actively engaged in the classroom, increasingly involved with the children in tutorial, small- and large-group sessions, and introduced to the necessary reflective activity of the developing teacher.

We felt the essential part of this program was learning how to teach through the apprentice model, the one we developed for the Scholars program. Our aim was to meld the practitioners' expertise with the expertise of university faculty.

In the afternoons, after the children had left, tenured faculty from Northwestern University, as well as Golden Apple Fellows, conducted coursework that would qualify as the courses required by Northwestern for teacher entitlement. This portion of the first phase related to the GATE interns' observations and experiences in the morning sessions.

WORKING WITH UNIVERSITY PARTNERS TO TRAIN ALTERNATIVE CERTIFICATION TEACHERS

The essential (and some argued radical) component to this part of our design was in proposing the partner university take the salient features of all its courses leading to teacher certification and weave them into a quilted, concomitant concept that would be presented to the interns over the course of a year.

The idea behind this structure was our belief that the traditional approach, while entirely appropriate for the eighteen- to twenty-two-year-old with limited knowledge of subject matter, scant knowledge of children, and growing concept of self, was not as appropriate for the adult. An adult—with knowledge of subject based on application of subject through employment; some stronger knowledge of children, having in many cases raised some; and with a stronger sense of self steeled by the years of adulthood—could begin to learn the craft of teaching through a different model.

In the traditional model, the compartmentalizing of the curriculum leading to teacher certification into separate and discreet courses only serves the function of time and convenience as perceived by the university. That construction does not help an adult learner develop a working, pragmatic knowledge of how to succeed in the classroom.

We believe that you learn about teaching concomitantly: philosophy and methods, for example, occur together in teaching instances; separate and discreet courses on both do not reflect the real world the teacher enters. So in Illinois in 1997, the only way an adult who desired a career change into teaching could achieve certification was to return to the world of the eighteen- to twenty-two-year-old and take more than two years of course work segmented and devised for the convenience of the university structure. The net result, we argued, was numbers of adults would not deign to offer their talents and experience to Illinois school children.

At the conclusion of the first phase, GATE interns are evaluated by both Golden Apple and Northwestern faculty. Those deemed successful are invited to the second phase of the program. Successful interns are hired to teach full-time in Chicago Public Schools at standard salary. Mentors would be assigned to the interns as part of the mentor program initiated by Chicago Public Schools. Northwestern and Golden Apple hire and prepare observers who, in addition to regular evaluation of teachers by school administrators, conduct frequent formal evaluations of GATE interns at their school site. Continuing course work is conducted by Northwestern faculty and Golden Apple Fellows in twice-monthly evening seminars.

A NONTRADITIONAL PATHWAY TO CERTIFICATION

This was the second radical concept in our proposal: that interns would be allowed to enter schools as teachers of record with a one-year license allowing them to do so granted by the state at Northwestern's recommendation.

The traditional pathway provides student teaching to its twenty-two-year-olds, a practice widely seen as, at best, inconsistent in offering a quality experience, and often plastic in its artificiality. Our core belief was that adults could continue to learn about and be successful with teaching while engaged in the art, properly mentored and observed. We also argued that adults engaged in apprenticeship models in all sorts of careers are compensated as adults, and we felt it appropriate to insist on full salary for interns employed in our program.

At the end of the school year, GATE partners, the university, the Golden Apple Foundation, and the school administration will convene to evaluate each GATE intern. Those deemed successful will be awarded certification.

The curriculum was co-designed by faculty of Northwestern University, which would guarantee that all of the GATE program's coursework would meet the requirements of Northwestern's coursework for teacher certification.

We claimed that through this program a competitive, intensive, selective, and demanding regimen, one that ultimately presents a high standard of teacher preparation for our targeted segment of the population, would be provided. Our initial assessment clearly demonstrated a need for high school math and science teachers in Chicago. We also maintained that the traditional pathway dissuaded women and men of quality who desired to be teachers in Chicago, and that we would actively seek out the best to participate in this initiative.

This time our path to launch a teacher preparation concept was rocky. As we sought approval in 1997 from the Illinois Teacher Certification Board, an arm of the Illinois State Board of Education, we were told in no uncertain terms such a concept was unappreciated. The concept of alternative routes to standard teacher certification, while common in other states, especially Texas, California, and Massachusetts, was thought anathema in Illinois.

There were clear reasons for this belief. The pathway to the classroom is guarded by both the two teacher unions and the deans of colleges of education in Illinois. Both were well represented in the Teacher Certification Board. I likened the experience to presenting an argument to the meat industry favoring increasing the consumption of fish in the populace. Our proposal was unanimously defeated.

We next sought a different pathway to allow this idea to begin. With the help of other partners, especially Pat Ryan, Jr. of the Inner City Teaching Corps (which sought certification for its interns teaching in Chicago Catholic elementary schools), we approached the state legislature seeking a bill that would allow us to begin our program. When I gave evidence at the Illinois Senate Education Committee on the merits of our proposal, I received both lavish praise and withering criticism for being so brazen as to concoct such an idea. The halcyon days of teaching Dante to seniors seemed simple indeed.

The net result of our effort was the passage of a bill in 1998 that became Illinois School Code 21–5b, allowing the GATE program to begin accepting candidates. Through the first three years of the program over 100 candidates have sought certification. Former scientists, engineers, a colorectal surgeon, attorneys ("recovering" lawyers, as they call themselves) have entered into teaching in Chicago. The candidates are fought over by Chicago high school principals who know of the reputation for quality in our candidates. They have successfully demonstrated the efficacy of our idea. In 2001 a second university, the University of Illinois at Chicago, joined with us to open another pathway for those wishing to teach elementary school children.

Since we began the GATE program, 11 other programs in alternative certification have been created in Illinois. Helping to solve the teacher shortage by utilizing the talents of this segment of society has been fruitful. In 2002, we examined 344 applicants for 50 openings.

TOWARD EXCELLENCE IN TEACHING

These ventures in teacher preparation have brought me close to those who desire to enter the teaching profession, despite its resource inequity, despite its low remuneration, despite the rancor and the disrespect associated with the profession. They enter determined to bring hope and sense and learning to children. They come with a belief that teaching transcends its travails to become an art form that requires tenacity, resilience, insight, acumen and, above all, hope. It has been an honor assisting them on their journey to the classroom. It has been an honor having the opportunity to place my beliefs about preparing for the teaching profession into practice through programs that have positively impacted the lives of 700 current or emerging teachers, a number that grows each year.

After the riots in Chicago during the 1968 Democratic National Convention, the Daley administration put out a documentary defending their actions entitled "What Trees Do They Plant?" While the film itself may have created varied opinions, its title always stuck with me as a benchmark in determining whether I or those I meet have done well with the legacy bequeathed to us.

When I was a young man and would complain about something, my father would say, "And do your arms move? Your brain, it works pretty good? Can your legs walk you to a better situation?" When I was a young teacher listening to the complaints of high school students, I would smile and nod sympathetically, then plan a future field trip to the Shriner's Hospital for Crippled Children in Chicago. One year, after watching the staff work with those wonderful children, and then listening to my students' quiet sniffling on the way back, one student looked up at me and said, "We haven't done anything with our lives."

"Not yet," I responded, "but there's still time."

I hold a great respect for the tree planters I have met in my life. The desire to find purpose in life by helping others find purpose in theirs is a blessed way to live. I have met people who command six-figure salaries who are totally unhappy with what they have contributed to life and are more than willing to move to a job that pays a fraction of what they earned, that provides all the frustration and challenge one can tolerate: public school teaching. And they are loving it. It is more than mere missionary zeal and more than mere masochism.

Done well, teaching is immensely rewarding. If you are deeply within it, keep a-going. If you are preparing to enter, hurry up and get in here. Children need you! If your heart is pure and your mind intent, the trees you plant will blossom.

Bibliography

Bettleheim, B. (1975). *The uses of enchantment: The meaning and importance of fairy tales.* New York: Vintage. ISBN 0679723935.

Brueghel, P. & Orenstein, N. (1989). *Pieter Brueghel the Elder.* New York: Metropolitan Museum of Art. ISBN 0870999915.

Calaprice, A. (Ed.). (2000). *The expanded quotable Einstein.* Princeton, NJ: Princeton University Press. ISBN 0691070210

Center for Urban Research and Development. (2001). Evaluation of the Golden Apple Foundation Scholars Program. Chicago: University of Illinois at Chicago.

Darling-Hammond, L. (1999). *Reshaping teaching policy, preparation and practice: Influences of The National Board for Professional Teaching Standards.* New York: American Association of Colleges of Teacher Education. ISBN 0893331686.

Eastwood, C. (Dir.). (1986). *Heartbreak ridge* [Motion Picture]. United States: Warner Brothers Films. ASIN 0790751186.

Greene, B. (1991, December 18). The price of Shanika's life. *Chicago Tribune*, p. 51.

Guest, J. (1993). *Ordinary people.* New York: Penguin. ISBN 0140065172.

Hawthorne, N. (1981). *The scarlet letter.* New York: Prentice Hall. ISBN 0553210092.

Hayakawa, S. I. (1949). *Language in thought and action.* New York: Harvest. ISBN 0156482401.

Hunter, M. (1994). *Enhancing teaching.* New York: Macmillan College Division. ISBN 0023589418.

Jung, C. (1981). *The archetypes and the collective unconscious.* Princeton, NJ: Princeton University Press. ISBN 0691018332.

Kidder, R. (1996). *How good people make tough choices: Resolving the dilemmas of ethical living.* New York: Fireside. ISBN 0684818388.

MacLeish, A. (1998). *J. B.: A play in verse.* New York: Mariner. ISBN 0395083532.

Mauris, J. (1990). *Rene Magritte: 1898-1967* [Big Art Series]. New York: TASCHEN. American Llc. ISBN 3822872156.

Murphy, F. (Ed.). (1990). *Walt Whitman: The complete poems.* New York: Viking. ISBN 014042226.

Puccini, G. (Comp.). (1995). *Puccini—Turandot / Sutherland, Pavarotti, Caballe, et al.* [CD], London. ASIN B0000041Q3.

Salinger, J. D. (1995). *A catcher in the rye.* New York: Lb Books. ISBN 0316769487.

Shapiro, K. J. (1978). *Collected Poems 1940-1978.* New York: Bantam. ISBN 039442543X.

Stevens, W. (1990). *The collected poems of Wallace Stevens.* New York: Vintage. ISBN 0679726691.

Walker, A. (1996). *The color purple.* New York: Pocket Books. ISBN 0671727796.

Warren, R. P. (1996). *All the king's men.* New York: Harvest. ISBN 0156004801.

Weir, P. (Dir.). (1989). *Dead poet's society* [Motion Picture]. United States: Buena Vista Films. ASIN 6301627768.

Wilder, T. (1998). *Our town.* New York: Harperperennial. ISBN 0060929847.

Wright, B. F. (Illus.). (1992). *The original mother goose.* New York: Running Press. ISBN 1561381136.

Zipes, J. (Trans.). (1992). *The complete fairy tales of the brothers Grimm.* New York: Bantam. ISBN 0553371010.

Index

as maps to classroom territory,
    17–18
history, 14
juxtaposition, 14
teacher's use of unkind, 14–15
uses, 13

Wright, B. F., 90
Writing exercises. *See* Reflective
    writing exercises, teacher

Zamora v. Pomeroy, 63

**CORWIN
PRESS**

The Corwin Press logo—a raven striding across an open book—represents the happy union of courage and learning. We are a professional-level publisher of books and journals for K-12 educators, and we are committed to creating and providing resources that embody these qualities. Corwin's motto is "Success for All Learners."